Lit Crit Guides

Reading and Interpreting the Works of

WILLIAM SHAKESPEARE

Walt Mittelstaedt

Enslow Publishing
101 W. 23rd Street
Suite 240
New York, NY 10011
USA

enslow.com

Published in 2017 by Enslow Publishing, LLC
101 W. 23rd Street, Suite 240, New York, NY 10011

Library of Congress Cataloging-in-Publication Data
Names: Mittelstaedt, Walt, author.
Title: Reading and interpreting the works of William Shakespeare / Walt Mittelstaedt.
Description: New York, NY : Enslow Publishing, 2017. | Series: Lit crit guides | Includes bibliographical references and index.
Identifiers: LCCN 2016005247 | ISBN 9780766079120 (library bound)
Subjects: LCSH: Shakespeare, William, 1564-1616--Criticism and interpretation--Juvenile literature. | Shakespeare, William, 1564-1616--Juvenile literature. | Dramatists, English--Early modern, 1500-1700--Biography--Juvenile literature.
Classification: LCC PR2895 .M628 2017 | DDC 822.3/3 [B] --dc23
LC record available at https://lccn.loc.gov/2016005247

Printed in the United States of America

Portions of this book originally appeared in *A Student's Guide to William Shakespeare.*

Shakespeare's text taken from the *Arden Shakespeare Complete Works* (1998, reprint 2014).

Photo Credits: Cover, p. 1 Stock Montage/Archive Photos/Getty Images; vectorgraphics/Shutterstock.com (series logo); p. 6 Heritage Images/Getty Images; p. 13 Stock Montage/Getty Images; p. 21 William Shakespeare/British Library, London, UK/ © British Library Board. All Rights Reserved/ Bridgeman Images; p. 25 Who said...? Ben Johnson and William Shakespeare (gouache on paper), Rainer, Paul (20th century)/Private Collection/© Look and Learn/Bridgeman Images; pp. 29, 139 Print Collector/Getty Images; p. 31 Claudio Divizia/Shutterstock.com; p. 34 G. Topham Forrest/ Wikimedia Commons/Blackfriars theatre conjectural reconstruction 1921.png/public domain; p. 39 © Dorling Kindersley ltd/Alamy Stock Photo; p. 48 Shakespeare, English School, (20th century)/Private Collection/ © Look and Learn/Bridgeman Images; p. 53 © North Wind Picture Archives; p. 56 Archive Photos/Getty Images; p. 60 Portrait of King Henry V (1387- 1422) (oil on canvas), Burnell, Benjamin (1769-1828)/Private Collection/Photo © Philip Mould Ltd, London/Bridgeman Images; p. 65 Universal History Archive/Getty Images; p. 73 Shakespeare performing at the Globe Theatre, Jackson, Peter (1922-2003)/Private Collection/ © Look and Learn/Bridgeman Images; p. 75 David Boyer/Getty Images; p. 84 Hulton Archive/Getty Images; p. 89 Oli Scarff/Getty Images; p. 99 Print Collector/Getty Images; p. 114 20th Century Fox/Getty Images; pp. 116, 133 Hulton Archive/Getty Images; p. 121 Manuel Litran/Getty Images; p. 127 Keystone-France/Getty Images; p. 150 Library of Congress; p. 153 Cole Burston/Getty Images; p. 159 Martha Holmes/The LIFE Images Collection/ Getty Images; p. 165 Shakespeare and his Friends at the Mermaid Tavern, 1850 (oil on canvas), Faed, John (1820-1902)/Private Collection/Bridgeman Images; p. 172 William Shakespeare, Nicholas Rowe, ed./Wikimedia Commons/Rowe Tempest.JPG/public domain; p. 179 Everett Historical/Shutterstock.com; p. 185 © AF archive/Alamy Stock Photo; p. 187 Julie Ainsworth/Folger Shakespeare Library Digital Image Collection/Wikimedia Commons Folger Reading Room.jpg/CC BY-SA 4.0.

Contents

William Shakespeare

The Bard of Avon

When legendary actor James Dean attended Indiana's Fairmount High School in the late 1940s, he was taught drama and speech by Mrs. Adeline Nall. Many years later, she recalled Dean asking her why she did not have the class do Shakespeare. Mrs. Nall answered, simply: "You're too young."[1] A year later, James Dean would go on to play Malcolm in *Macbeth* at UCLA. It would be his only brush with Shakespeare in his tragically short acting career.

Mrs. Nall's view is still common today, which is unfortunate, because the work of Shakespeare can appeal to audiences of any age or background. This is most evident in modern theater and filmmaking, where Shakespeare's works are borrowed often. For example, the classic musical *West Side Story* follows the plot of Shakespeare's *Romeo and Juliet* almost exactly. More recently, the film *O* (2001) places Shakespeare's *Othello* in a high school basketball setting. There is also the Oscar-winning film *Shakespeare in Love* (1998), which imagines some of the biographical details of Shakespeare's life. Actor and director Kenneth Branagh has produced very popular films of Shakespeare's plays: *Henry V* (1989), *Much Ado About Nothing* (1993), *Hamlet* (1996), and *As You Like It* (2006). Director Baz Luhrmann updated the story of Romeo and Juliet in *Romeo + Juliet* (1996), starring Leonardo DiCaprio and Claire Danes. More recently, three fine film versions of *The Merchant of Venice* (2005), starring Al Pacino, and *Romeo and Juliet* (2013), starring Douglas Booth and Hailee Steinfeld, and *Macbeth* (2015) starring Michael Fassbender and Marion Cotillard have appeared.

Indeed, it would seem there is no end to Shakespeare's influence and appeal. It is for this reason Shakespeare is known as the "Immortal Bard of Avon."

Shakespearean Themes

Shakespeare's plays were first divided into the categories of comedy, history, and tragedy in 1623 by his fellow actors, John Heminges and Henry Condell, in the first collected edition of his plays, the First Folio. They used "history" to refer to plays like *Richard III* and *Henry V*. Previously, histories had been considered tragedies. Certain other plays were also later categorized as romances. Within Shakespeare's large body of work, there are many different themes. Perhaps the most frequent of these is the theme of universal order.

Shakespeare and Order

Basic to an understanding of Shakespeare's work is the concept of order to the Elizabethans. Keep in mind, it had not been much more than a century before Shakespeare's

Shakespeare Rates

In a poll of historians taken by the A&E Cable Television Network for its Biography of the Millennium program in 2000, Shakespeare placed fifth in overall impact on the world around him among celebrated personalities of the past thousand years. Shakespeare was just ahead of Christopher Columbus and one behind Charles Darwin. No doubt, Shakespeare would have been pleased by the panel's top pick—Johannes Gutenberg, inventor of the printing press.

time that England had been devastated by the Wars of the Roses—a time when no monarch could be certain of holding power for very long. In fact, it was not until the Tudor dynasty that stable rule was established. Even then, Mary Tudor and Edward Tudor had short reigns. Only with the Accession of Elizabeth in November 1558 (six years prior to Shakespeare's birth) would England finally enjoy a long reign by a popular monarch.

theme

A distinctive quality or concern in one or more works of fiction.

Thus the idea of a preserved order was very important to the people of England in Shakespeare's day. This idea underlies not only the plays based on English history that Shakespeare wrote but other genres as well, including comedy. Comedy typically ends with union and concord—usually in the form of a marriage, with the traditional "happily ever after" ending.[2]

Order in the Histories

The Wars of the Roses (1455–1485) were portrayed by Shakespeare, wholly or in part, in four of the ten history plays he penned in the 1590s. In fact, he had just finished the last of the history plays, *Henry V*, when he wrote his first Plutarch-derived Roman tragedy, *Julius Caesar*. It may not be coincidence that *Caesar* has the same general theme as the plays dealing with English history. When Caesar was assassinated in 44 BC, Rome was plunged into civil war.

Of course, there are certain themes unique to individual histories. *2 Henry IV* and *1 Henry VI*, for example, are concerned with betrayal as much as rebellion.[3] And in *Henry V*, Shakespeare is less concerned with betrayal and rebellion than he is with the nature of kingship.

Order in the Comedies and Romances

Shakespeare's comedies commonly deal with first love and marriage. Marriage is the end result, either real or promised, no matter how gloomy things seem for the lead couple at the start of the play. Two of Shakespeare's funniest comedies, *The Comedy of Errors* and *A Midsummer Night's Dream*, both have very somber openings, but nevertheless, they end to almost everyone's satisfaction. Because the comedies deal largely with love and marriage, heroines tend to play a more significant role in them than in the histories or the tragedies.[4] Over and over, Shakespeare will take a one-dimensional woman from his source and convert her into a memorable character.

Shakespeare also shows something of an interest in twins in his comedies. Twins, of course, made an excellent device for creating disorder via identity confusion. In *The Comedy of Errors*, written at the outset of his career, he wrote about two sets of twins, adding an extra set that his source did not have. In mid-career, Shakespeare again takes up the subject of twins—this time a brother and sister—in *Twelfth Night*.

In the comedies, Shakespeare is simply saying that life goes on, despite any complications or threats that face us. It does so because love will not be denied, whether opposed by stubborn parents or sneaky rivals. Order is always preserved.

The romances were not recognized as a dramatic genre until long after Shakespeare's time. The romances blend tragedy and comedy and, like the comedies, end happily with a marriage. But the going from start to finish involves many ups and downs, sometimes to the point of death. Even so, there is reunion and renewal at the end and the love has overcome all the obstacles placed in its path.

Order in the Tragedies

Shakespeare's four main tragedies deal with a noble nature beset with jealousy (*Othello*); ambition and moral collapse (*Macbeth*); fulfillment through sorrow (*King Lear*); and the evils attending revenge (*Hamlet*). Other tragedies make use of these themes, if only to distort them, as *Antony and Cleopatra* does with ambition. Cleopatra and Lady Macbeth notwithstanding, the tragedies focus mainly on complex male characters.

Shakespeare's Verse: Not So Blank

Understanding Shakespeare on his own terms is often difficult for new readers. But daunting as it may seem, one must acquire the feel of Shakespeare's verse in order to fully appreciate the value of his works. Hearing Shakespeare's verse spoken comes across as conversational and much less bewildering than when one first encounters it on the printed page.

Blank Verse

"No, no, we haven't the time. Talk prose," says the owner of the Rose playhouse, Philip Henslowe, to Will Shakespeare at the beginning of the much-acclaimed film *Shakespeare in Love*. Henslowe may not have known it, but blank verse is not so time-consuming as he makes it out to be. Three centuries later, playwright George Bernard Shaw would insist that it was the easiest thing in the world to write—or at least, easier to write than prose.[5] And in Shakespeare's hands, it appears so. When the Nurse makes her first speech in *Romeo and Juliet*, she speaks blank verse—but when the printers published the First Folio of Shakespeare's plays in 1623, they printed the speech as prose because it read so naturally to them.

Doubting Shakespeare

The idea that someone other than William Shakespeare of Stratford-on-Avon could have written the plays and poems known as the Works of William Shakespeare is an old one. This Authorship Controversy goes back to the late eighteenth century and may even go back to some satirical verses written in Shakespeare's own lifetime.

Early skeptics leaned toward Sir Francis Bacon as the true author of the Works. This is because it seemed unlikely to some that anyone but a learned individual could have acquired the kinds of experience reflected in Shakespeare's plays and poems. In fact, the Reverend James Wilmot, late in the eighteenth century, had conducted his own research into Shakespeare's life in Warwickshire and ended up burning his notes. He was convinced that Bacon was the poet behind the Works. His research and beliefs were kept secret until the Shakespearean scholar Allardyce Nicoll found them in 1932 and announced them to the world.[6]

But Bacon would be only one of a field of more than sixty claimants held to be the true author. In recent decades, Edward de Vere, the seventeenth Earl of Oxford, has been the leading claimant. He was praised by Francis Meres for his comedies in 1598.[7] His initials can be found signing several poems in anthologies such as *England's Helicon* (1600). In addition to his writing ability, Oxford also sponsored an acting company.

The Authorship Controversy will likely long continue, but it should be noted that no substantial evidence shows that there was doubt about Shakespeare's authorship of the works that go by his name in his own day and that it was nearly two centuries afterwards before anyone really did have any doubts about it.

Sir Francis Bacon is one of many who have been considered to be the "true" Shakespeare. None of the theories has ever been proved.

As we all know, Shakespeare's plays make use of a variety of verse forms as well as prose. If Shakespeare wanted to work in a fourteen-line sonnet, as he did at times in *Love's Labour's Lost*, or if he wanted to add a three or four verse song, as he did in all of the comedies, he would do so without hesitation. But this type of thing was the exception with him. He usually dealt in blank verse.

blank verse

Unrhymed iambic pentameter.

foot

In poetry, a unit of a stressed and unstressed syllables.

Blank verse was a sixteenth-century English invention that had its start before Shakespeare was born. Blank verse is unrhymed and is almost always written in what is known as iambic pentameter. Iambic pentameter is a line of poetry consisting of five "feet," with each "foot" made up of two syllables or beats. (So one line of iambic pentameter would have ten syllables.) Each foot starts with an unstressed syllable, followed by a stressed syllable. To better understand stresses, consider one of Shakespeare's most famous lines (from *Hamlet*): "To be or not to be." Which words do you stress when you read this line out loud? The natural stresses should fall on the words "be" and "not." It should be read as: "to BE or NOT to BE." This is natural iambic form—starting with the unstressed syllable and following with the stressed. If you tried reading it the opposite way—"TO be OR not TO be"—it would sound stilted and unnatural.

Elizabethan playwrights, including Shakespeare, varied their lines of iambic pentameter with a foot that might be *trochaic* (the stress going before the unstressed syllable), *anapestic* (two unstressed syllables preceding a stressed syllable), the *spondee* (two stressed syllables in a row), or some other combination. Writers in Shakespeare's time would often try to rewrite the rules of artistic expression. The full line we just cited from *Hamlet*, for example, actually has an extra (eleventh) syllable: "To be or not to be, that is the question." When there is an unstressed syllable at the end of a line of verse, it is called a feminine ending.

iambic

A metrical foot of poetry or verse that has an unstressed syllable preceding a stressed syllable.

pentameter

A line of poetic verse possessing five metrical feet (ten syllables).

Literary Devices

Shakespeare, in his plays and poems, uses a variety of literary devices. These devices include similes and metaphors, symbolism, personification, imagery, puns, oxymorons, hyperbole, and alliteration.

Similes and Metaphors

A simile compares things indirectly. The giveaway in dealing with similes is the use of "like" or "as." This is an example of one of Shakespeare's similes (from *Othello*):

> She was false as water. (5.2.134)

Metaphors compare things directly. Something *is* something else. Possibly the most famous speech in *As You Like It*, that of the cynic Jacques embodying the seven ages of man, is metaphoric throughout:

> All the world's a stage,
> And all the men and women merely players;
> . . . Seeking the bubble reputation
> Even in the cannon's mouth. (2.7.139–140; 153–154)

Hamlet describes the corruption of his world in this way:

'tis an unweeded garden
That grows to seed, things rank and gross in nature
Possess it merely. (1.2.135–137)

Personification

Personification is another means of comparison. It invests inanimate objects with human qualities. In *Hamlet*, Claudius says:

. . . and our whole kingdom
To be contracted in one brow of woe (1.2.3–4)

Romeo pictures the daytime as having legs:

Night's candles are burnt out, and jocund day
Stands tiptoe on the misty mountaintops. (3.5.9–10)

Symbols

Symbols give a universal significance to individual objects. In *Hamlet*, Shakespeare brings up one of his favorite themes—the importance of majesty in holding a nation together—by comparing the king to a wheel. Rosencrantz tells King Claudius that:

The cess of majesty
Dies not alone, but like a gulf doth draw
What's near it with it. Or it is a massy wheel
Fix'd on the summit of the highest mount,
To whose huge spokes ten thousand lesser things
Are mortis'd and adjoin'd, which when it falls,
Each small annexment, petty consequence,
Attends the boist'rous ruin. (3.3.15–22)

Rosencrantz is referring to Claudius's importance to Denmark, but we, the audience, find it more appropriate to think of the late king, Hamlet's father, as the object of his speech.

Richard III, in the play named after him, is referred to as "a dog," "a toad," "a spider"—all of which symbolize his harmful effect on the realm of England. Macbeth sees a dagger in his frenzied mind, which symbolizes ruin to the state. Later on, he mentions the "twenty trenching gashes in Banquo's head," which further emphasizes the moral chaos following the death of King Duncan.

alliteration

The repetition of words beginning with the same consonant.

spondee

A metric foot consisting of two stressed syllables.

trochaic

A metric foot possessing a stressed syllable before an unstressed syllable.

Imagery

Images of sense, color, and sound are sprinkled throughout most speeches in Shakespeare's plays. Sea imagery, for example, is especially predominant in those later plays known as the romances—*Pericles*, *Cymbeline*, *The Winter's Tale*, and *The Tempest*. This is natural since these plays usually involve journeys and a considerable passage of time.

Hamlet is full of varied imagery—mirrors and glasses depicting the differences between illusion and reality, as well as images of warfare, disease, and poisoning, all tending to show the disrepair of Denmark in the hands of the usurper Claudius. There are also theatrical images found in the phrases "antic disposition," and "cry of players," and in such words as "prologue," "play," and "puppet." These words and phrases point up the central importance to the story of the play-within-a-play called *The Murder of Gonzago*, which depicts the murder of Hamlet's father by Hamlet's uncle.

Wordplay in Shakespeare

Shakespeare's masterful way with words has made him the envy of writers for centuries. But then, he came from an era that loved words. English in the Elizabethan age was still flexible enough to enlist new words, either foreign words or *neologisms* (so-called coined words, made up by writers on the spot). Edmund Spenser gave us the word "derring-do" in *The Faerie Queene*. A stuffy Cambridge don named Gabriel Harvey gave us such useful words as "amicable," "jovial," "idea," "addicted," and "ingenuity." Thomas Nashe endowed our language with such words as "indictment," "infringement," "eligible," and "destitute."

symbol

Something that stands for, represents, or suggests another idea or thing.

What Shakespeare contributed most memorably were useful expressions. Thanks to him we speak of "breathing one's last" and "falling to blows." It is due to him that we "drink healths" and consume "dishes fit for the gods." Indeed, without Shakespeare, we could not even "catch a cold." The word "conveyance" is Shakespeare's, as is "eventful."[8]

Puns

Shakespeare made wide use of puns in his plays. A pun is that form of wordplay wherein a joke is made out of words that have the same sound (and perhaps even the same spelling) but different meanings. The pun was a favorite device of the era, but Shakespeare reveled in it even more than his contemporaries. Critics of later periods sometimes held Shakespeare's liberal use of the pun against him. Dr. Samuel Johnson, for instance, called puns Shakespeare's "fatal Cleopatra."

Romeo and Juliet leaps to mind when we think of Shakespeare's puns and quibbles. The play has some 175 quibbles.[9] And when we think of puns and quibbles in this play, we think chiefly of Mercutio. Even his fatal wound cannot prevent him from making one last pun: "Ask for me tomorrow and you shall find me a grave man" (3.1.97–98). Later in the play, Romeo puns on the word "fly." When he speaks of his banishment, he says, "Flies may do this, but I from this must fly" (3.3.41).

One of the most interesting instances of Shakespeare's wordplay comes from *Hamlet*. Hamlet is speaking to Polonius, the courtier, whom Hamlet knows to be an ally of his enemy, King Claudius. He wants to know about Polonius's acting in his university days:

> HAMLET: What did you enact?
> POLONIUS: I did enact Julius Caesar. I was killed i' th' Capitol; Brutus killed me.
> HAMLET: It was a brute part of him to kill so capital a calf there. (3.2.104–108)

Besides the play on the words, brute/Brutus and capital/Capitol, there could well be a further meaning. If the usual dating of Shakespeare's *Julius Caesar* and *Hamlet* is correct—with the former dated 1599 and the latter, two years later—then it is not unlikely that the part of Caesar in the first play was played by the actor who played Polonius in the latter play. Also, the actor who played Brutus might then have played Hamlet.[10]

Oxymorons

An oxymoron is the placing of two words side by side that have opposite meanings. Romeo, in his lovelorn days with Rosaline before he meets Juliet, is in love with love. One figure of speech that is predominant with him in his early moments is the oxymoron.

> O heavy lightness, serious vanity,
> Misshapen chaos of well-seeming forms,
> Feather of lead, bright smoke, cold fire, sick health,
> Still waking sleep, that is not what it is! (1.1.178–181)

In *A Midsummer Night's Dream*, there is a meaningful oxymoron in stage manager Quince's lines in the first act:

> Marry, our play is, *The most lamentable comedy and most cruel death of Pyramus and Thisby*. (1.2.11–12)

SHAKESPEARE IN PRINT

Shakespeare's plays, when they were gathered up by his colleagues in 1623, were published in what is called the First Folio. Four Shakespeare Folios appeared in the course of the seventeenth century. When Shakespeare's plays were printed individually (and only half of them were in his lifetime), they were published as quartos or octavos. These were smaller (or, at least, thinner) than folios, probably printed in smaller numbers and certainly more easily lost. It did not help matters that their covers were paper (softback).

Technically, folios were books printed from sheets that were folded in half. Each leaf made two separate pages. The pages are 7 × 9 inches. Quartos were printed from sheets folded twice, making four separate pages. Octavos were printed from sheets folded three times, making eight pages. The page size is similar to that of a modern paperback. Only a few of Shakespeare's plays and poems were printed in octavo format.[11] The most famous octavo of the period is Francis Meres's *Palladis Tamia* (1598).

These lines make use of the oxymoron, "lamentable comedy," and, on the whole, poke fun at the bookselling profession of the day with their overly long titles.

Sibilance

A poetic device used by Shakespeare when he wished to paint a tender scene or express a quiet thought is sibilance. Sibilance is a gathering of *s* sounds in the space of a line or two. Romeo does it best:

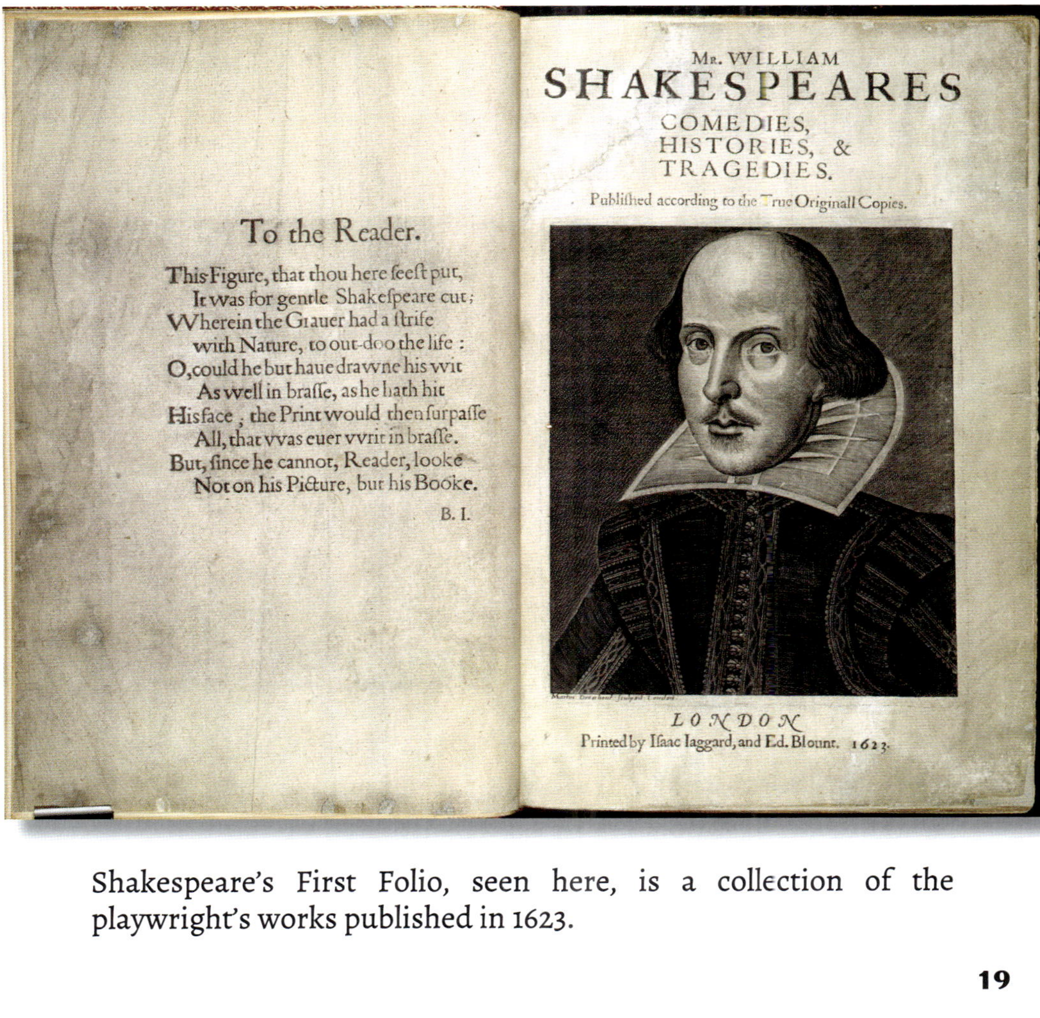

Shakespeare's First Folio, seen here, is a collection of the playwright's works published in 1623.

How silver-sweet sound lover's tongues by night,
Like softest music to attending ears. (2.2.165–166)

When one reads lines like this, one has to think that Shakespeare wrote *Romeo and Juliet* (and *A Midsummer Night's Dream*) when the experience of writing his greatest poetry was fresh upon him—that is, at the time he had written "Venus and Adonis," "The Rape of Lucrece," and at least some of his sonnets.

Repetition

Repetition is a good way of getting someone's attention. Shakespeare works his word magic through the simple device of repetition, sometimes merely repeating a powerful word a number of times. Hamlet, in his discourse with the Ghost, hears of Claudius's villainy and shouts:

O villain, villain, smiling, damned villain! (1.5.106)

In *King Lear*, the tragic hero-king gives vent to a heart-wrenching, agonized repetition of a single word that can hardly be improved upon for getting instant sympathy:

Never, never, never, never, never. (5.3.307)

Shakespeare's Characters

The great and near-great are the lead characters of such tragedies as *King Lear*, *Hamlet*, *Julius Caesar*, and *Antony and Cleopatra*. In these plays, Shakespeare depicts the tragic fall of kings, princes, and those who would rule the world. But it is not just the tragedies that trade so much in royalty. It may be found throughout Shakespeare. In the comedies and late romances, kings and queens can be found, though not always as the leads.

In other tragedies, such as *Romeo and Juliet* and *Othello*, Shakespeare is interested in exhibiting love when it is opposed by feuding families or by one lone villain. In these tragedies, the main characters are usually more common folk, or what we might consider today as middle class. Shakespeare was not the first among the dramatists of that day to portray the conflicts of lesser classes, but his portrayals were the most interesting and memorable of the era.

Whether dealing with royalty or middle-class burghers, Shakespeare's plays always introduce a number of characters from the working class. Bottom and his semi-literate confederates in *A Midsummer Night's Dream* are of the first order of this type. So, too, is the cobbler in *Julius Caesar*. In fact, in at least one play, *Love's Labour's Lost*, the minor characters all but run away with the play.[12] The characters nearly all belong to

Ghost Characters

Shakespeare's plays, in their early, unedited form, present us with a number of curiosities. One of the most interesting has to do with so-called ghost characters. This term refers to those persona in the text who do nothing, say nothing, and are not noticed by the rest of the cast. Examples of ghost characters include Innogen in *Much Ado About Nothing* and Violenta in *All's Well That Ends Well*. How these characters got there is a good question. It may be that Shakespeare originally intended to flesh out these characters and lost interest, leaving them to remain in a stage direction of his text to puzzle scholars for the rest of time. Or it may be that Shakespeare changed the names during composition and did not go back and cross out the original names.

different historical periods, but Shakespeare molds them into Elizabethans.

Shakespeare Criticism

Shakespeare's works were popular in his own day. His contemporaries often praised him. These tributes took the form of simple allusions that, at first, acknowledged some work, usually a poem. Later, the tribute took the form of imitation. Shakespeare's plays and poems often served as the inspiration for a work by another writer.

At times, however, some of Shakespeare's contemporaries would criticize his work. One of these critics was his friend Ben Jonson. In his writings and conversations, Jonson dealt with Shakespeare's work more than any other of the poet's contemporaries. Jonson could be critical of Shakespeare at times, since he himself was a devoted student of classical writers who obeyed the ancient rules of drama—rules that Shakespeare often violated.

After Shakespeare's death, a new situation developed in England. Shakespeare's plays were gathered together in the Folio, a handsome, expensive volume containing thirty-six of his plays. This book kept Shakespeare's fame and reputation alive during the turbulent decades that followed its publication. In fact, the volume (with various modifications) underwent four editions between 1623 and 1685.

allusion

A seemingly incidental mention of something that is, in reality, designed to hint at a much deeper meaning.

Following the English Revolution, Shakespeare underwent a distinct loss of reputation. One reason for this was that the new drama that thrived in the Restoration period was composed mostly of rhyming couplets. Shakespeare, who could write prose and poetry equally well, tended to use too much prose and too many low characters for Restoration tastes. Such dramatists as John Dryden and William Davenant undertook adaptations of some of Shakespeare's plays, leaving them hardly recognizable to us.

couplet

Two successive lines of verse that are joined in some way (usually by rhyme).

In the eighteenth century, Dr. Samuel Johnson edited an edition of *Shakespeare* (1765) and wrote a very influential preface to it. His insights are still quoted today. His remark about Shakespeare's love of puns and quibbles as "his fatal

An illustration depicts Shakespeare with his friend Ben Jonson.

Cleopatra for which he was content to lose the world" is perhaps his most quoted remark.

Shakespearean criticism began to truly flower in the twentieth century. At the beginning of the century, A. C. Bradley offered psychological investigations of Shakespeare's four great tragedies—*Hamlet*, *Othello*, *Macbeth*, and *King Lear*. The writings of Sigmund Freud were also brought increasingly to bear on Shakespeare's works by a number of critics as the century wore on. More and more, these views influenced stage productions such as John Barrymore's *Hamlet* in the 1920s. Former actor turned director and critic, Harley Granville-Barker brought this background to his Shakespeare criticism as found in his *Prefaces to Shakespeare* (1927) and *More Prefaces to Shakespeare* (1946).

Interest in Shakespeare, incredibly enough, only seems to be growing. It would seem that as long as the English language is spoken, Shakespeare's works will be read and performed. In this light, the Bard of Avon is indeed immortal.

The Age of Shakespeare

If Shakespeare had lived and written in some other period of history, what would he have amounted to? If he had been born a century earlier or later, would he have been as great? It is easy to picture him living in the nineteenth century, writing stuffy novels or in Hollywood during the Golden Age earning a good living writing screenplays but remaining unknown to the general public because he did not choose to direct those scripts. Somehow, Shakespeare happened to be born in just the right time—a time that perfectly suited his remarkable gifts.

The Elizabethan Age (1558–1603) in which Shakespeare lived and wrote was an era given to great extravagance. It knew no bounds. It chafed at limits and restraints. No shore was too far for ships to sail; no thought too unattainable for expression. It was an era that produced many great artists and musicians, as well as great explorers and adventurers.

Extravagance was obvious in the clothing that the Elizabethans and Jacobeans wore. Everything was padded. The ladies could not help but boast a narrow waistline since their wire-hooped farthingales ballooned outward from the hips down. Men wore padded peascod doublets, though, as a general rule, by Elizabeth's reign, these were toned down from the ridiculous proportions that they had previously assumed. And always, men and women alike affected the giant ruff at the neck, starched for better effect.[1]

This extravagance, so pronounced in their clothing, could be seen in other aspects of Elizabethan life, too. When it came to language, for example, the Elizabethans pulled out all the stops. They would make compounds of Greek and Latin words or simply invent completely new words of their own.[2] They even invented a new dramatic genre—the chronicle (or history) play.[3]

It was in the midst of this era that the greatest writer in the history of the English language was born.

Young Shakespeare

William Shakespeare was born in Stratford on or about April 23, 1564, and died on what was likely his fifty-second birthday, April 23, 1616. He was buried on the twenty-fifth. Though he was the oldest of the five Shakespeare children who survived infancy, only his sister Joan outlived him. She would die thirty years later. Her line, in fact, survives. Her descendants—the Hart family—can be found today living in Australia.[4]

We could only wish that Shakespeare had recorded much of his fifty-two years in a diary or that he simply had dispatched a few letters, full of dates and facts and figures, and that some of these had come down to us. Unfortunately, the innermost self of the greatest poet in the English language forever eludes us. We can only deduce a few details from such seemingly personal works as his sonnets or other writings.

A great mass of legend surrounds Shakespeare's early life. There are stories about his poaching deer from a park down the road from Stratford and, afterward, getting himself soundly whipped for it and locked up overnight. Another colorful tale has young William engaged in a drinking contest at a neighboring town. Afterward, he supposedly fell asleep

Queen Elizabeth was a great supporter of Shakespeare, who often performed his dramas at court.

under a nearby mulberry tree, forever after honored as "Shakespeare's Canopy."[5]

At some point in his youth, Shakespeare took an interest in acting. Acting troupes passed through Stratford in his early years and needed permission of the poet's father, John, the town's bailiff (equivalent to a mayor), to act out their plays at the town hall. It may be that on one of these visits, the acting company known as the Queen's Men needed an actor (to replace member William Knell, who had been killed in a duel).[6] But there is little to connect Shakespeare with the Queen's Men. Judging by evidence provided by the title pages of his early published plays, he was more likely to be a member of Pembroke's or Sussex's Men. Shakespeare's youngest brother, Edmund, and Charles Hart—a probable nephew—were also actors.[7]

What Shakespeare's education was may be guessed. As the son of a town official, he was entitled to admission into the free school at Stratford. The grammar school boy pictured by Romeo in *Romeo and Juliet* sounds like firsthand experience:

> Love goes toward Love as school boys from their books,
> But Love from Love, towards school with heavy looks.
> (2.2.156–157)

Shakespeare in London

Just when Shakespeare came the eighty miles from Stratford to London is unknown. Certainly, he would not have left his native Stratford during the early days of his marriage, when his children—first Susanna and then the twins, Hamnet and Judith—were born. Some time after 1585 seems the likeliest occasion for his leaving home. Although he was named in a lawsuit concerning his mother's inherited property (called Asbies) in the summer of 1587, he need not have been on

Shakespeare was born in this house in Stratford-on-Avon and lived here until after he was married.

hand for that action. Following 1585, the next seven years in Shakespeare's life are a complete blank and have come to be known as the "lost years."

According to eighteenth-century tradition, Shakespeare began his theatrical career by holding horses outside the London playhouses. As one might expect, whatever he put his mind to, he excelled at and in no time, he was the leader of the group of horse-holders called "Shakespeare's boys." This tale is often incorrectly attributed to Dr. Samuel Johnson who, because of his stature as a Shakespearean editor and critic, gave the story its legs.[8]

It may well be that Shakespeare's first attempts at playwriting are all but unrecognizable to us today. A scene in this or that play or a character to help a play along might be all that he contributed. The old play, *Sir Thomas More*, which for centuries had lain around as a manuscript in the British Library, may well be an example of Shakespeare's early work. This play contains a hundred lines that many scholars feel sure are in his handwriting.[9]

Not until Shakespeare was twenty-eight is there any mention of him in print. In a letter to three fellow dramatists, buried in his novella *A Groatsworth of Wit* (1592), Robert Greene makes a sneering, though somewhat veiled, reference to a certain "Shake-scene." "Shake-scene" is probably Shakespeare (though it is possible that the actor Edward Alleyn is meant). From this point forward, until his death nearly twenty-four years later, scholars have little trouble keeping track of Shakespeare.

Shakespeare's first published work, one he referred to as the "first heir of my invention," was an erotic poem called *Venus and Adonis*. It carried a dedication to the young Earl of Southampton, Henry Wriothesley (pronounced RISEly

SHAKESPEARE FROM TEXAS?

What has to be the most amusing allusion to Shakespeare the movies have so far given us occurs in *Dodge City* (1939). When the film's hero, Errol Flynn, and his sidekick, Alan Hale, see young "Babs" Watson holding horses, Flynn asks Hale, "Wasn't it Shakespeare who began by holding horses?" Hale asks, "Who?" "William Shakespeare," Flynn replies. "I never heard of him. What part of Texas is he from?" Hale asks. "Stratford-on-Avon," says Flynn, resignedly.

or ROSEly). It was printed by Richard Field, a man born in Stratford and whose family had business dealings with the Shakespeares. Field was a successful stationer and it may be in his shop that Shakespeare found many of the sources that he relied on for his work at this period. Shakespeare demonstrates, for example, a knowledge of George Puttenham's *The Arte of English Poesie* (1589), and Field was the printer of this book.[10]

During these years, while Shakespeare was busy in London, his wife, the former Anne Hathaway, and their three children would have stayed in Stratford. Anne was eight years older than her husband. The couple lost their son Hamnet in August 1596 when he was eleven. It is thought that the characters of Mamillius in *The Winter's Tale* and young Arthur in *King John* may owe something to Hamnet.

There is no record that shows that Shakespeare's family lived with him at any time while he lived in London. There is not even talk of a visit by them. Apparently, Shakespeare traveled to Stratford to keep up contact with his family and his business interests. Shakespeare probably came to Stratford during the summer each year, when travel was easiest, and at such other times as his theatrical activities would permit. Records show that he had business dealings at home throughout his London career.

It may be that Shakespeare's marriage, after the birth of the twins, did not require much togetherness or, more likely, that he was married to his work. In twenty years he wrote some forty plays, not to mention the 154 sonnets and various poems. Some plays, like *The Comedy of Errors* and *The Tempest*, are short, but they still require two hours to perform. (*Macbeth*, another short play, was shortened, quite possibly, for a performance at court before a sleepy King James, who might nod off

Shakespeare and his company performed here at the Blackfriars Theatre. Because it had a roof, it was used as a winter playhouse.

at intervals during a performance.[11]) Short plays or long—*The Winter's Tale* needs three hours to perform and *Hamlet* at least four—Shakespeare remained productive for a span of nearly two decades.

In these years, Shakespeare was an extremely busy man. Not only was he writing plays and poetry, but he was also acting in these plays as well as others. He probably directed plays as well. As a sharer in his company's profits, he would have been responsible for some of the upkeep of the playhouse(s), too. He would have overseen productions and acquired stage properties such as the "ass-head" mentioned in the stage directions to the Folio version of *A Midsummer Night's Dream*. He may even have had to sweep the floor from time to time!

Like many industrious and ambitious young people, Shakespeare was well paid for his work. (By 1597, he was able to buy the best house in Stratford, the home of a former Lord Mayor of London, Sir Hugh Clopton.) As a repertory company, the Lord Chamberlain's/King's Men would have been putting on old plays as well as acquiring new ones at the rate of seventeen a year.[12] Of course, Shakespeare was the main provider of new plays by his company.

The Blackfriars

In 1608, Shakespeare's acting company (now the King's Men) acquired the Blackfriars playhouse, an indoor playhouse. The Blackfriars originally had been a monastery in west central London, not far from the city's business center. This enclosed playhouse shared duties with the company's open-air playhouse, the Globe, which lay south of the Thames River.

The Blackfriars, a private playhouse, accommodated a more refined and cultivated audience than the Globe and other

Playhouses and Acting Companies

When Shakespeare came to London around 1587, there were only a handful of playhouses. They were the newly erected Rose, the Theatre, the Curtain, the Blackfriars, a number of inns, and Paris Garden, which was the site of animal-baiting spectacles sometimes used to put on plays. The most famous theater of all time and the one habitually associated with Shakespeare—the Globe—would not be built until the summer of 1599.[13] The playhouses resided in districts called liberties, which were areas free from the jurisdiction of the London authorities and under the Queen's control.

Because of her delight in having plays put on at court, Elizabeth was not about to persecute the actors, provided they could prove the patronage of some noble in the realm. As we might expect, Elizabeth herself sponsored an acting company, the Queen's men, which was the leading acting company in the 1580s. (The fortunes of this company seem to have dwelt in one man, the great comedian of that day, Richard Tarleton. When he died in 1588, just after the defeat of the Spanish Armada, the fortunes of the Queen's men took a downward spiral.)[14]

Among the companies thriving at the end of the 1580s were Leicester's men, the Lord Admiral's men, Sussex' men, and the Lord Strange's men—the troupe that later became the Lord Chamberlain's/King's Men, the company to which Shakespeare belonged.[15]

outdoor playhouses. Even a different mode of transportation was used by playgoers to attend this private playhouse. The playhouses south of the river were reached either by crossing London Bridge from the north on Gracious Church Street or traveling by boat down the Thames. But the Blackfriar's catered to a crowd that generally arrived in that new form of transport—the horse and carriage.

With a change of playhouses and audiences came a change in the kind of plays that Shakespeare wrote. Younger dramatists, such as John Fletcher and Francis Beaumont, were in vogue at this time and Shakespeare quickly got in step with them. He fashioned a series of wild, improbable dramas, half comedy, half tragedy, which are called the romances by critics of a later day. These plays—*Pericles, Cymbeline*, *The Winter's Tale*, *The Tempest*, and *The Two Noble Kinsmen* along with the history *Henry VIII*—were the last plays that Shakespeare would write.

Back to Stratford

Toward the end of The *Tempest*, Prospero says:

> I'll break my staff,
> Bury it certain fathoms in the earth
> And deeper than did ever plummet sound
> I'll drown my book. (5.1.54–57)

These famous lines are viewed by many as Shakespeare's personal farewell to the stage. *The Tempest* is usually thought to have been written in 1611–1612 and by May 1612, he was again living in Stratford, after two decades in London. Prospero's oft-quoted words in this play may indeed be what the poet hoped would stand as his valedictory to drama, but, if so, it was not to be.

Pocahontas

Shakespeare probably never met a Native American, but a number of his plays, early and late, mention the Americas and Native Americans. Had Shakespeare lived a little longer, he may have met Pocahontas. After all, his good friend, Ben Jonson, did. The occasion was an entertainment called a masque, which Jonson provided for King James and Queen Anne at their court at Whitehall in 1617. Pocahontas had married an English tobacco planter, John Rolfe, and took a new name, Rebecca. She became quite a celebrity in England. She died later that year, just as she was getting started on a trip to visit her homeland, Virginia.

Sometime before June 29, 1613, Shakespeare would write *Henry VIII*, and probably earlier that same year he was putting the finishing touches on *The Two Noble Kinsmen*, a play believed to be largely the work of John Fletcher. As a matter of fact, Shakespeare was in London in March 1613, acquiring property near the Blackfriars. He may have contributed to *The Two Noble Kinsmen* at this time.

Shakespeare was to live out his remaining years in Stratford. In May 1612, we know from legal documents that he was in London to testify in a lawsuit between two of his friends, Stephen Belott and Christopher Mountjoy, concerning the amount of a dowry. At this time, he signed his name to a deposition and that signature went unnoted from that moment until 1908 when a University of Nebraska professor and his wife discovered it in the Chancery of the Public Records Office in London. In point of chronology, it is the first of Shakespeare's six surviving signatures.[16]

This monument to Shakespeare in Stratford was erected not long after his death.

It would seem that the last few weeks of Shakespeare's life were hard on him. On February 10, 1616, his younger daughter, Judith, married Thomas Quiney. This assuredly was a festive occasion and legend has it that two of Shakespeare's fellow poet/dramatists, Ben Jonson and Michael Drayton, were with him. The trio may have celebrated the nuptials a little too freely since Shakespeare is supposed to have contracted a fever as a result and died two months later.

Shakespeare died on what was apparently his fifty-second birthday, April 23, 1616. In August 1623, Shakespeare's widow, Anne, died. In November 1623, the First Folio was published. In the preface, we learn that the monument to Shakespeare in Stratford had been erected sometime between his death in April 1616 and November 1623, when the Folio came out.

The Poems and Sonnets

Two long narrative poems, each filling a small paperback book, were the first works by William Shakespeare to be published. These poems appear to have been written at a time when the London theaters were closed due to a severe outbreak of the plague. Whether these poems were the first things written by Shakespeare is not known.

Shakespeare's non-dramatic poetry dates from 1593 on. He began by writing his two longest poems—narrative poems based on stories by the Roman writer Ovid and Roman historian Livy. Shorter poems followed over the next decade. The 154 sonnets were probably written during this same period. Shakespeare's sonnets were the last of his poems to be published. One reason for this may have been the long period of time Shakespeare took to compose them (from the early 1590s to more than ten years later). Another reason that the sonnets were published so late in Shakespeare's career may have to do with their personal subject matter. Because of this, Shakespeare may not have been anxious to see them released.

Venus and Adonis

When Shakespeare wrote the two long narrative poems *Venus and Adonis* and *The Rape of Lucrece*, Ovid's influence was widespread. In 1589, Thomas Lodge had published *Scylla's Metamorphosis*. This book was based on Ovid's epic, *The Metamorphosis*, which deals with Greek mythology and was written in the first century CE. Shakespeare not only picked his subject from Lodge but also the meter of *Venus and Adonis*. The poem consists of six-line stanzas made up of a quatrain (a four-line stanza) and a couplet (a two-line stanza), rhyming ababcc, in iambic pentameter.

Venus and Adonis is twelve hundred lines long, the second longest of Shakespeare's poems (after *Lucrece*). The poem deals with the love of the goddess Venus for a youth named Adonis. Shakespeare, with his notorious sense of humor, tells the story like a comedy. Early on (line 30), for instance, Venus pulls the retiring Adonis from his mount and both tumble to the ground like football players.

Because of its titillating mix of lust and seduction, along with stressing the need for procreation (something underlying the sonnets as well), *Venus and Adonis* fits right in with the erotic poetry cycles of the 1590s. Though Shakespeare provides marvelous descriptions of a horse and a hare, it is the poem's erotic tone that lingers in the reader's memory. For this reason, if no other, *Venus and Adonis* was very popular with young people.

Venus and Adonis went through nine editions in Shakespeare's lifetime, beginning with the first edition of 1593. A tenth edition came out in 1617, the year after Shakespeare's death. This is quite a track record—better, in fact, than that of his most popular plays, *Hamlet*, *Richard III*, and *I Henry IV*.

The Rape of Lucrece

The Rape of Lucrece is written in rhyme royal (seven-line stanzas, rhyming ababbcc)—so named because King James I tried his hand at this verse form. The poem was Shakespeare's second attempt at serious literature. Like *Venus and Adonis*,

Lucrece was dedicated to the young Earl of Southampton. It was printed by Richard Field in May 1594.

The Rape of Lucrece went through just half the number of editions that *Venus and Adonis* had by 1640. The reason for this might lie in the fact that the latter poem is much more a moral exercise than the former and young readers strongly favored the tone of *Venus and Adonis* to the stern moralizing of *Lucrece.*[1]

stanza

A portion of a poem divided from the larger poem via a recurring pattern of meter or rhyme.

Lucrece is set in the last days of the Roman monarchy in 509 BCE . Certain Romans at the siege of an enemy town, not far from Rome, wager as to which of their wives is the most virtuous. Collantine, the husband of Lucrece, turns out to be the winner. Tarquin, who has lost the wager, is the son of the tyrant currently ruling Rome. Having seen Lucrece, he is overcome with desire. He goes to Collantine's home, is entertained graciously by Lucrece, and then proceeds to ravish her. Lucrece goes into a long lament, which exposes Tarquin to both her husband and father. This incident sparks the overthrow of the Roman monarchy and replaces it with the republic.

His falchion on a flint he softly smiteth
That from the cold stone sparks of fire do fly
Whereat a waxen torch forthwith he lighteth,
Which must be lodestar to his lustful eye;
And to the flames thus speaks advisedly:
"As from this cold flint I enforced this fire,
So Lucrece must I force from my desire."

Here pale with fear he doth premeditate
The dangers of his loathsome enterprise,

And in his inward mind he doth debate
What following sorrow may on this arise;
Then looking scornfully, he doth despise
His naked armor of still-slaught'red lust
And justly thus controls his thoughts unjust;

"Fair torch, burn out thy light, and lend it not
To darken her whose light excelleth thine;
And die, unhallowed thoughts, before you blot
With your uncleanness that which is divine.
Offer pure incense to so pure a shrine,
Let fair humanity abhor the deed
That spots and stains love's modest snow-white
weed." (lines 176–196)

These three stanzas out of the poem's two hundred and sixty give some idea of the verse type employed by Shakespeare in *The Rape of Lucrece*. He would return to it in a later poem in the so-called "complaint" tradition—*A Lover's Complaint*. Note that Shakespeare enforces "sparks" with the unnecessary "of fire" (pointless since sparks are always of fire). Nevertheless by doing so, he gives some idea of the extreme lust inside Tarquin. Somehow, a simple "spark" does not sound as hot as a "spark of fire."

Tarquin's internal debate shows him to be a complex villain. The first two lines of the third stanza, moreover, make use of an image found in *Romeo and Juliet*: "O, she doth teach the torches to burn bright" (1.5.47). Quite possibly, the two works were written close together in time.

The wearisome part of the 1,855 lines of *Lucrece* has to do with involved soliloquies ("disputation") by Tarquin before he commits his crime and afterward; as well as Lucrece's lamentations before she commits suicide. Nevertheless, there are signs of the great dramatist Shakespeare was to become in Tarquin's soul-searching. There is also a hint of Prince Hal (later, King Henry V) in Brutus, who is reputed to be a fool but throws off this facade to rouse Collantine to seek revenge.

The Passionate Pilgrim

The Passionate Pilgrim was published in two editions in or around 1599. A third edition followed in 1612. All three editions of this poem were published by William Jaggard, a publisher with a somewhat checkered history.[2] Very few copies of any edition of this minor poetry are known and the earliest is known only through a fragment. Shakespeare had written his contributions to the volume earlier in the decade. These contributions include two sonnets and a song from *Love's Labour's Lost* and two other sonnets (which would later appear in somewhat different form as numbers 138 and 144 in the *1609 Sonnets*). Other poems in the collection are by Christopher Marlowe, Richard Barnfield, and Bartholomew Griffin. There is a reply by Sir Walter Raleigh (so most scholars think) to the poem by Christopher Marlowe.

The Phoenix and Turtle

In 1601, a collection of poems dedicated to Sir John Salusbury was published under the title *Love's Martyr: Or, Rosalin's Complaint, Allegorically shadowing the truth of Love, in the constant Fate of the Phoenix and Turtle*. Generally, it is simply called *The Phoenix and Turtle*. In addition to the namesake poem of the title—"Love's Martyr," by Robert Chester—it had poems by Shakespeare, Ben Jonson, John Marston, and George Chapman. All the poems treated a single theme. Shakespeare's entry is called "The Phoenix and Turtle." The turtle in this poem refers to the turtle dove. The phoenix is the bird of legend that lived for several hundred years before dying in a burst of flames, only to return to life by rising from its own ashes.

"The Phoenix and Turtle" is a short "poetical essay" of sixty-seven lines, written in iambic tetrameter (lines of four metrical feet) in thirteen quatrains (four-line stanzas), followed by a threnody (a poem or song lamenting death) in iambic trimeter (lines of three metrical feet) in five tercets (three-line stanzas). It is Shakespeare's most difficult and unusual poem. Two verses from the Threnos, spoken by Reason, follow:

> Beauty, truth and rarity
> Grace in all simplicity
> Here enclosed in cinders lie.
>
> Death is now the phoenix' nest,
> And the turtle's loyal breast
> To eternity doth rest.

In this poem, the turtle is male and represents constancy. The phoenix is female and represents beauty, truth, and rarity.[3] The poem celebrates the undying love and unity of the phoenix and the dove. The union of the two defies reason in that they are so completely one. Thus, two are one and love transcends reason—a major theme of the comedies. This identity of the phoenix and the turtle is reminiscent of something Hamlet says in a play, written at just about the same time (circa 1601). In the fourth act, Hamlet refers to the king as his "mother."

> King: Thy loving father, Hamlet.
> Hamlet: My mother—father and mother is man and wife, man and wife is one flesh, and so, my mother. (4.3.50–54)

There is a villain of sorts in "The Phoenix and Turtle"—the Eagle—but, by and large, all good birds are urged to gather to commemorate the beauty of the selfless love between the dove and phoenix.

Sonnets

Shakespeare's most famous poems are undoubtedly his 154 sonnets. The sonnet form originated in Italy in the twelfth century, flowering in its primary function as love poetry, first with Dante in the late thirteenth and, most famously with Petrarch, in the fourteenth century. When Shakespeare wrote his sonnets in the 1590s, nearly every poet who wielded a pen wrote sonnets. The sonnet has a history of being a personal composition. It is commonly associated with the love of a man for a woman (although Lady Mary Wroth turned this notion around a decade after Shakespeare, when a woman declared her love for a man in a sonnet).

In *Love's Labour's Lost*, written around 1594–1595, Don Armado is so taken with Jaquenetta that he swears that he will "turn sonnet." Scholars generally feel that *Love's Labour's Lost* was written around the time Shakespeare wrote the sonnets. In fact, sonnets by the poet are worked into the fabric of this play.

Shakespeare's sonnets concern a number of things. For one thing, Shakespeare can be heard punning on his name in the "Will"

tercet

A poetic stanza or group of lines that is three lines in length.

tetrameter

A line of poetic verse possessing four metrical feet (eight syllables).

trimeter

A line of poetic verse possessing three metrical feet (six syllables).

Sonnets—135, 136, 143, and possibly 134. His lot as an actor, if we are to believe these poems, wass an unhappy one. He refers to his "outcast state" in one of the most famous sonnets of the sequence—Sonnet 29. He has a young friend and he and the young friend are interested in the same woman. This woman is deceitful, at least in Shakespeare's eyes, and has acquired a nickname over the years from scholars: the dark lady. She may

This illustration depicts Shakespeare writing in his study. He often worked on more than one play at a time.

THE SONNET

Sonnets became a widespread verse form in Italy in the fourteenth century. The Italian poet, Petrarch, wrote poems to a lady that he idealized after no more than glimpsing her. The lady was named Laura and the poems that praised her were sonnets. Petrarch's sonnets were fourteen lines long, consisting of an eight-line stanza (the octave), complemented by a six-line stanza (the sestet). In England, in the middle of the sixteenth century, the verse form caught on, thanks to Henry Howard, Earl of Surrey, and Thomas Wyatt, who had traveled on the continent and brought the verse form back to England.

As usual, Shakespeare tried his hand at the art form and left a distinct impression. Like all the English sonneteers, Shakespeare employed a fourteen-line stanza of iambic pentameter, which consisted of three four-line stanzas (quatrains) and a terminating couplet. His rhyme scheme was confined to each quatrain as abab cdcd efef gg. Poet Edmund Spenser also dealt in the sonnet form, employing a different rhyme scheme to his "Spenserian" sonnets. Spenser's rhyme pattern goes abab bcbc cdcd ee. From this we can see that one rhyme is carried over from one quatrain to the next, resulting in a concluding rhyming couplet.

have been someone well known to Shakespeare, perhaps even an obscure literary figure of the time, such as Emilia Lanier. We do not know who this dark lady was, but we shall always wonder.

Whether the sonnets are autobiographical or mere literary exercises has been debated since the rediscovery of these poems in the late eighteenth century. By the beginning of the twentieth century, Sir Sidney Lee had just about persuaded everyone that Shakespeare was not being autobiographical in his sonnets (although he still recognized the youth in the sonnets as the real-life Earl of Southampton).[4] Today, most commentators on the sonnets find that they tell a story that is true, at least in its broad outlines.

Shakespeare spends the first seventeen sonnets urging his young friend to marry. In this way, his good looks will live forever in his children. (This same theme crops up in many of Shakespeare's plays, particularly the comedies.) There is a rival poet in the sonnets (78–86), whose reputation is formidable. Shakespeare is even a little daunted by him. Both poets seek the patronage of the young man. Shakespeare speaks of missing his young friend in some sonnets; in others he accuses the youth of betraying him with the dark lady.

octave (or octet)

A poetic stanza or group of lines that is eight lines in length.

In one of the best-liked sonnets (29), Shakespeare feels that his profession has cut him out of the youth's circle of friends. This theme is repeated in sonnets 36, 110, and 111. Age is a problem, too. Shakespeare remarks on his age a number of times, although he was only in his thirties when most or all of the sonnets were written. Sonnet 73 is Shakespeare's masterpiece on this theme (and perhaps any theme). Sonnet 138 repeats this age theme.

(Sonnet 138, by the way, is one of few sonnets that can be accurately dated, since it appeared with Sonnet 144 in *The Passionate Pilgrim* in 1599.)

There are twenty-six sonnets addressed to the dark lady. Shakespeare does not reveal much about her except that she is married—though not happily. Two of the weaker sonnets end the sequence and are devoted to Cupid.

Perhaps Shakespeare's most famous sonnet (18) was addressed to the youth:

Shall I compare thee to a summer's day? *a*
Thou art more lovely and more temperate. *b*
Rough winds do shake the darling buds of May, *a*
And summer's lease hath all too short a date. *b*
Sometimes too hot the eye of heaven shines, *c*
And often is his gold complexion dimmed; *d*
And every fair from fair sometimes declines, *c*
By chance or nature's changing course untrimmed. *d*
But thy eternal summer shall not fade *e*
Nor lose possession of that fair that thou ow'st; *f*
Nor shall Death brag thou wanderest in his shade, *e*
When in eternal lines to time thou grow'st. *f*
So long as men can breathe or eyes can see, *g*
So long lives this, and this gives life to thee. *g*

Shakespeare's sonnets make use of three quatrains followed by a couplet; fourteen lines in all. They differ from the Italian (or Petrarchan) sonnet, which divides its fourteen lines into an octave (eight-line stanza) and a sestet (six-line stanza). Note the bravado displayed in the concluding couplet, where Shakespeare boasts that his words will live forever—as long as "men can breathe or eyes can see." This is known as a conceit and was a common device of poets at the time. It is similar to modern rappers bragging about their "mic skills" in their songs today.

4 Shakespeare's History Plays

The English chronicle or history play hadn't really been established when Shakespeare took it in hand after the defeat of the Spanish Armada in the summer of 1588. A tidal wave of patriotism swept over England following this epochal event. Playwrights, such as Robert Greene and Christopher Marlowe, among others, wrote history plays, but no one mastered this type of drama like William Shakespeare.

It may be that Shakespeare cut his dramatic teeth on the history play. Certainly the pattern of image clusters found in *1 Henry VI* suggest that it is a very early play, since images are more neatly worked in the fabric of the two later *Henry VI* plays.[1]

So new was the history play that of the six tragedies by Shakespeare listed by Francis Meres in his *Palladis Tamia* (1598), four are what we now call histories—*Richard II*, *Richard III*, *King John*, and *Henry IV* (a two-parter, known to Meres as one play). It would take the publication of the First Folio in 1623, however, to distinguish between Shakespeare's tragedies and histories.

Shakespeare seemingly tired of the history play after 1599 with *Henry V*, perhaps his greatest achievement in the form. He did not write another history play until the very end of his career when he wrote *Henry VIII* (quite possibly with the assistance of John Fletcher).

The First or Minor Tetralogy

The three parts of *Henry VI* and *Richard III* make up Shakespeare's first or minor tetralogy. A tetralogy is a series of four connected works. These four plays were written, most probably, between 1590 and 1595. By the latter year, the final two parts of *Henry VI* had been published in "bad quartos"—that is, in a form very different from how we know them today and with different titles. For this tetralogy, as with most of his plays dealing with English history, Shakespeare relied primarily on Raphael Holinshed's *Chronicles of England, Scotland and Ireland* (second edition, 1587) as well as Edward Hall's *Union of the Two Noble and Illustre* [illustrious] *Families of Lancaster and York* (1548).

The 1588 British defeat of the Spanish Armada, pictured here, was cause for great optimism throughout the country.

The subject matter of the minor tetralogy deals with the Wars of the Roses, which has its beginning in the rose garden scene (2.4) in *1 Henry VI*. The Wars of the Roses were an English dynastic conflict wrapped up inside the Hundred Years War, which took place between England and France during the latter half of the fourteenth and the first half of the fifteenth centuries (1337–1453).

Shakespeare, in the three *Henry VI* plays, presents an England divided by factions with no firm ruler. Henry VI is a child in the first play and a weak adult in the other two. He is killed at age fifty in the third part of the trilogy bearing his name and his funeral appears in *Richard III*. In the three plays in which he appears, Henry is presented as ineffectual and easily manipulated by those around him. On the other hand, Henry is likable in his aversion to worldly ambition and power—he is religious and philosophical, a direct forbear of Richard II in the second tetralogy.

The motif of the "uneasy crown" is a favorite in Shakespeare's plays based on English history. His kings, more often than not, envy the common run of people who seem to not have a care in the world.

> O, God! methinks it were a happy life
> To be no better than a homely swain;
> To sit upon a hill, as I do now,
> To carve out dials quaintly, point by point . . . (*3 Hen. VI*, 2.5.21–24)

One reason for the regret on their part is their heavy burden of responsibility. A king must keep order in his realm and Shakespeare's English kings are always beset with civil war. Henry VI, of all the English kings, had it the worst. On top of the lengthy Wars of the Roses, there was Jack Cade's rebellion. Of short duration, Cade's rebellion was successful, insofar as Cade actually crowned himself king. These scenes takes place in Act Four of *2 Henry VI*.

As Cade is a Kentish peasant, boarish and uneducated, Shakespeare can relish him. Rustics, as we see so often in the plays, delighted Shakespeare, and Cade gives him a chance to evoke a little humor in the midst of the Wars of the Roses, following the death of the Duke of Gloucester, brother to Henry V. But Cade, though an illiterate buffoon, is sinister, too. His followers threaten to plunge England into a state of anarchy, worse even than civil war.

tetralogy

A series of four connected works.

"The first thing we do, let's kill all the lawyers," Dick recommends to Cade (4.2.74). Cade seconds the motion and would hang all clerks (symbolic of educated professionals) with their inkhorns around their necks.

To make Cade more monstrous and threatening, Shakespeare took events out of the Peasant's Revolt of 1381, during the reign of Richard II, and combined them with Cade's rebellion.[2] These incidents involved burning the law schools—known as the Inns of Court—and trying to destroy London Bridge. Cade's rebellion thus amounted to a civil war wrapped up inside a civil war (the Wars of the Roses). Shakespeare uses Cade as an appendage of Richard, Duke of York. In his view of English history, he was always anti-Yorkist. This was prudent when Elizabeth sat on the throne since she was herself descended from the Lancastrians, the enemies of the Yorkists. Elizabeth's grandmother, however, was Elizabeth of York, daughter of Edward IV. It was the marriage of Elizabeth's grandmother to Henry Tudor that ended the Wars of the Roses.

Ironically, the strong ruler that eventually arrives on the scene is himself a monster: Richard III, son of Richard, Duke of York in the *Henry VI* plays. He is Shakespeare's first great villain. He is not yet one of Shakespeare's most fully developed dramatic figures, however, since he is rather one-dimensional in his villainy. He always plots, owing loyalty to himself alone. No character in the rest of the Shakespearean universe, not even Macbeth or Iago, is so completely evil. He needs no one else unless to manipulate him.

> And this word "love," which graybeards call divine,
> Be resident in men like one another
> And not in me: I am myself alone. (*3 Henry VI*, 5.6.81–83)

Shakespeare recites his work for the court of Queen Elizabeth.

Richard III may be the first of Shakespeare's plays to make use of imagery connected with the acting profession. These images suggest the contrast between appearance and reality. They figure the hypocrisy that Richard undergoes to get what he wants.[3]

The Second or Major Tetralogy

Shakespeare continued his study of English history, begun in the first tetralogy, with the second or major tetralogy. The four plays in this group are *Richard II*, *1 Henry IV*, *2 Henry IV*, and *Henry V*. Unlike the earlier tetralogy, no one has ever doubted that Shakespeare was the sole author of these works.

Their dates—like dates connected with most plays by Shakespeare—are hard to pin down, precisely. Except for *Henry V*, they were probably well in hand in time for the Garter festivities of April 23, 1597, when Shakespeare's acting company's patron, Lord Hunsdon, was inducted into the Knights of the Garter with the queen herself present. (Lord Hunsdon, George Carey, was her cousin.) *Henry V* must have been ready about the time Lord Essex went to Ireland to subdue rebellion in the summer of 1599, since the Chorus to Act V clearly has his anticipated return. At any rate, *1 Henry IV* was registered for publication on February 25, 1598. *Richard II* was already published by then; both *2 Henry IV* and *Henry V* were in print by 1600.

The Inimitable Henriad

The Henriad part of this tetralogy—the two *Henry IV* plays and *Henry V*—gives us two of Shakespeare's most memorable characters—Prince Hal (later, King Henry V) and Sir John Falstaff. Hal is Shakespeare's most perfect hero and is described as the "mirror of all Christian kings" (*Henry V*, Chorus, 2.6).

Falstaff is the "fat knight," who is the cause for wit as much as mirth in others and quite possibly the most remarkable comic creation in the English language.

The first play in the second tetralogy is *Richard II*. It was written around 1595—during that highly lyrical period when Shakespeare was writing *A Midsummer Night's Dream*, *Romeo and Juliet*, the sonnets, and *Love's Labour's Lost*. Richard is one of Shakespeare's most poetic and idealistic kings. He is duly seated on the English throne, but his poetic temperament qualifies him for some other less hard-nosed profession. As a hero, he could be a lot better—he steals land from a rival—but he could be a whole lot worse. We like him in death:

> How, now! What means death in this rude assault?
> Villain, thy own hand yields thy death's instrument.
> [Snatching an ax from a SERVANT and killing him.]
> Go thou, and fill another room in Hell.
> [He kills another. Then Exton strikes him down.]
> That hand shall burn in never-quenching fire
> That staggers thus my person. Exton, thy fierce hand
> Hath with the King's blood stained the King's own land,
> Mount, mount, my soul! Thy seat is on high,
> Whilst my gross flesh sinks downward, here to die.
> (5.5.105–112)

1 & 2 Henry IV form the middle part of the Lancastrian tetralogy. The two *Henry IV* plays use material from Shakespeare's favorite historian, Raphael Holinshed, and comical scenes largely unhistorical and spun mostly from Shakespeare's own imagination. It is a successful mix, since these plays, especially "Part One" have always been among Shakespeare's most popular plays. The setting is England in the early part of the fifteenth century. The action is rebellion from the north and west against the rule of King Henry IV.

The Fat Knight—Sir John Falstaff

Sir John Falstaff dominates virtually every scene he is in. Legend reports that the queen herself had asked Shakespeare to do a comedy showing Falstaff in love. Shakespeare, so the story goes, responded with *The Merry Wives of Windsor.*

Falstaff is old (his age fluctuates twenty years between the two *Henry IV* plays), but he feels young. That is his charm and therein lies his guile. Whether Falstaff is a coward is one of the most critical points about his character and has been debated since the eighteenth century. As he has it: "The better part of valor is discretion"(*1 Hen. IV*, 5.4.118–119).

Falstaff is a mocker and a scoffer. He mocks his betters, such as the Lord Chief Justice, who is an honest, if somewhat rigorous, man. Falstaff also runs afoul of Sir John (the prince's brother) and the prince, himself, and he scoffs at such basic values as responsibility and honor. He also possesses a quick and sarcastic wit:

> Prince: I see a good amendment in thee—from praying to pursetaking.
>
> Falstaff: Why, Hal, 'tis my vocation, Hal. 'Tis no sin for a man to labor in his vocation. (*1 Henry IV*, 1.2. 108–109)

Notice that Falstaff speaks in prose. His knack for figurative language shows him to be a poet in prose. Falstaff, like Bottom in *A Midsummer Night's Dream*, surrounds himself with members of the lower classes. For this reason, he speaks prose characteristically, even as they do.

Falstaff is the prince's merry companion, but it is evident from their first scene together that a time will come when the

Shakespeare's *Henry V* tells the story of the English king who successfully battled France in the Hundred Years War.

prince will have to go his own way. However, it takes nearly two whole plays for this to happen and for that we are thankful.

Themes of the Henriad

Both *Henry IV* plays deal with rebellion. In both the king is victorious, but in the sequel (if we may call it such), the king dies and the prince ascends the English throne as King Henry V.

These two plays deal with the theme of order as essential to a realm if it is to thrive and the opposing of appearance and reality. King Henry IV, after all, is a usurping king, not a duly ordained one. His rule is at bottom an act, an impersonation of a king. His remorse for this is genuine, however, unlike Falstaff's continuous outpourings of reform. The wild Prince Hal is another instance of appearance versus reality in these plays. He throws off his disguise completely at the end of *2 Henry IV*, but, of course, we have seen his regal self all along.

Henry V continues the story of Prince Hal, now "King Harry" or Henry V. The play takes place mostly in France. In this history, Shakespeare gives us his idea of the perfect ruler. He is brave and his feet are planted firmly on the ground. We have seen him in the two previous histories consorting with rascals and due to that fact, he now knows how to rule them. In one remarkable scene in this play, Henry goes among his troops in disguise to learn what is on their minds (4.1). The king has some fun while in disguise setting up a tiff between the gallant Fluellen and the loudmouth Williams. This may be for fun on his part, but it shows both the King and us what mettle the English soldiers were made of that went over to France to win the Battle of Agincourt in 1415.

The Last History: *Henry VIII*

Henry VIII was Shakespeare's last history play and very nearly his last play. *The Two Noble Kinsmen* is probably later and, like *Henry VIII*, was probably co-authored by John Fletcher. This history is not one of Shakespeare's most popular plays—there are few memorable speeches or juicy parts. Despite this fact, it was one of the first, if not the first, Shakespeare play to be filmed.[4]

There is a good reason for this. It contains plenty of spectacle. There is a meeting of monarchs in the first scene (the French king and Henry). There is a trial scene (Katherine of Aragon's) in act 2, scene 4. The splendor of Anne Boleyn's coronation takes place in first scene of act 4. There is a vision by the deposed Katherine of Aragon in which she is crowned with bay leaves by six figures in white in a masque (4.2). Finally, following the christening of Elizabeth Tudor, there is Archbishop Cranmer's prophesy looking forward to the reign of Elizabeth (5.4).

Conclusion

Shakespeare finished his career with *Henry VIII*, a history play written long after his other histories and full of declamations and spectacle but not about much of anything. It is a play of episodes, in which, by the way, he finds time to bring in an unblushing allusion to a Native American with quite a history (5.3.34). More than anything else it is a tribute to the great queen, who, by then, had been dead ten years.

In his history plays, Shakespeare wished to depict how England prospered under strong rulers and suffered for years to come under weak and vacillating ones. Assassination, even of a weak ruler (Richard II, Henry VI), is evil.

The plays on English history give way to romantic comedy at the end of the 1590s. They sport villains, but death is held at arm's length. Their chief aim is to end happily, usually in a marriage. They are thus the golden or "happy comedies." *Twelfth Night* is considered the peak of Shakespeare's achievement in this line.[5]

5 Shakespeare's Comedies

An early legend has Shakespeare teaching in a rural school before coming to Stratford. If true, it explains a few things. Such a position would give him the background in the Roman writers that he calls upon in his earliest writing. Plautus, Ovid, and the historian Livy are drawn upon by Shakespeare for his two narrative poems and *The Comedy of Errors*.

Though scholars differ as to whether Shakespeare's first play was a history play or a comedy or even the tragic *Titus Andronicus*, there can be no doubt that *The Comedy of Errors* is an extremely early work. Part of the reason for this has to do with sources. The play looks like Shakespeare is keeping one eye on his source—the play *The Menaechmi* (the twins, Manaechmus)—as well as the *Amphitryon* of Plautus, as he is writing. To be sure, he adds to Plautus's complications, tacking on an extra set of twins to the proceedings just to make certain his comedy has enough to do (and untangle) by the time the two hours are up. Though the play is mentioned a number of times in Shakespeare's lifetime, it did not appear in print until after his death, with the publication of the First Folio.

Two other comedies, *Love's Labour's Lost* and *The Two Gentlemen of Verona*, also appear to be early works. We can try guessing their order, but only one thing about them is certain: They were all written by 1598 when they are mentioned by Francis Meres in *Palladis Tamia*.

The Comedy of Errors was one of Shakespeare's earliest works.

For his early comedies, Shakespeare looked to an ancient Roman playwright, Renaissance Italian storytellers, and—in the case of *Love's Labour's Lost* and *A Midsummer Night's Dream*—to his own fertile imagination.[1] His plots thrive on mistaken identity brought about by men donning disguises to impersonate other men (*Taming of the Shrew* subplot) or women dressing as men (Julia in *The Two Gentlemen of Verona*) or by a country yokel delivering a letter to the wrong party (Armado's letter to Jaquenetta and Berowne's to Rosaline in *Love's Labour's Lost*).

It is clear, then, that much of the action in these early comedies depends on mere chance rather than any defects of character. Not that chance does not play a part in tragedy—it is all over the place in *Romeo and Juliet* and *Hamlet*—but we look for it more readily and to a larger extent in comedy. This is especially true in what we consider Shakespeare's earliest comedies, where character does not so much drive the action of the play as in Shakespeare's mature comedies. When comedy is all chance or accident driven and not character driven, it is said to be farce.

The Comedy of Errors and *The Taming of the Shrew* are examples of early Shakespearean farces; *The Merry Wives of Windsor* is an example of one written in mid-career. Later comedies, like *Much Ado About Nothing* and *Twelfth Night*, also rely a great deal on chance, but before we think of the accidents of chance that befall the heroines and heroes of these plays, we think of their personalities. In these latter plays, character governs the action—that of Benedick and Beatrice in *Much Ado* and of Olivia and Viola in *Twelfth Night*. In fact, in these latter plays, it is the women who govern most everything.[2]

As mentioned, in *The Comedy of Errors*, Shakespeare trumped his source by revolving his play around two sets of twins instead of one. Also, one of the twins is married. Add to this the separation of the twins for a number of years and then a reunion, and accident becomes inevitable. In this farce, Shakespeare is trying out issues with which he will deal later.

Shakespeare deals with the transforming power of love to overcome any adversity, especially in his comedies. Happy endings are sometimes pulled out of the jaws of death in his comedies—*The Comedy of Errors* and *A Midsummer Night's Dream* are just two such. The sentence hanging over old Aegeon's head in the earlier play leads us to wonder if things can possibly turn out right. In *The Comedy of Errors*, chance also makes for trouble. In *A Midsummer Night's Dream,* the rough spots are mostly character driven—somebody loves somebody and somebody else is left out—but chance is there in the form of Puck's mistaken anointing of Lysander's eyes with the love philtre in act 2, scene 2.

Also early in Shakespeare's career was *The Taming of the Shrew*. This play has always been a favorite on the stage and its relationship to another play of that day with a strikingly similar title, *The Taming of a Shrew*, is still a mystery. In Shakespeare's play, much depends upon the way Katherina (the "shrew") is played. If she is seen as too subservient to her husband at play's end, modern audiences are apt to take offense. A more subtle approach showing her as "tamed" and not to be trusted at the same time has gained the most representation in our day.[3] This attitude is reinforced by Lucentio's skeptical comment at the end of the play. ("'Tis a wonder, by your leave, she will be tam'd so.")

Shakespeare's early comedies make use of a number of devices that he will later use in the so-called "golden comedies" at the turn of the seventeenth century—the happy trio of *As You Like It*, *Much Ado About Nothing*, and *Twelfth Night*. In the early comedy *The Two Gentlemen of Verona*, Julia dresses as a page to follow the fickle Proteus from Verona to Milan. This anticipates Viola's dressing as the page, Cesario, to be in the company of Duke Orsino, whom she loves. Julia, in her pursuit of her man, is also reminiscent of Helena in *All's Well That Ends Well*, a later, "dark" comedy.

It is interesting, too, that both *Love's Labour's Lost* and *A Midsummer Night's Dream*, written we think at around the same time, make use of rustics providing entertainment to be commented upon by their betters. This reflects the fact that the author of these two plays was an actor accustomed to theatrical conventions, one of which was the privilege that aristocrats could sit on the stage as a play was being acted and comment on the action. (Ben Jonson and Beaumont and Fletcher occasionally made use of this device as well.)

The early comedies in one way, at least, are different than the later comedies. Though they might occasionally have a remarkable song in the text, as does *Love's Labour's Lost*, with its songs by the owl and the cuckoo, songs generally are more frequent in the later comedies. There, they are more carefully integrated to character and a play's theme.[4]

The Golden Comedies

After finishing his last great cycle of English history plays—and having had some fun doing Falstaff in love at Elizabeth's command, according to legend—Shakespeare turned once more to comedy.[5] And what comedies he produced at the end of the sixteenth century: *As You Like It*, *Much Ado About Nothing*, and *Twelfth Night* mark the zenith of Shakespeare's comic vision. Shakespeare must have turned out these comedies in quick profusion, one after the other. It would not have been difficult for him to do so. As we have seen, much of what he would do in his later comedies he had already tried out in his earlier comedies. Disguises worn by women to impersonate men and characters eavesdropping on someone else's private conversation had been utilized in *The Two Gentlemen of Verona* and *Love's Labour's Lost*.

farce

A comedy that is driven by chance or accident.

As You Like It

Shakespeare returns to the "green world" in *As You Like It*. The main setting, the Forest of Arden, probably did not exist apart from Shakespeare's fertile imagination. There are no fairies in it, as in the enchanted wood outside Athens in *A Midsummer Night's Dream*. It is a good world, where one can meditate or fall in love with ease. The wood has a serpent and a lioness, but such exist only to renew the natural bond of brotherhood between Orlando and Oliver, when the former saves the latter's life. There are no less than four marriages in this play and two reconciliations. It is Shakespeare's busiest comedy.

The main plot involving Orlando's estrangement from his older brother, Oliver, is paralleled by the subplot of the usurping Duke Frederick, who has pulled the rug out from beneath Duke Senior, father to Rosalind and the rightful power in the land. Like *A Midsummer Night's Dream* a few years earlier, the action involves a journey from the court to the woodland and back to the court.

It is instructive to see how Shakespeare diverged from his sources in this play. For example, Shakespeare's immediate source for *As You Like It*—Thomas Lodge's story *Rosalynde*—

does not make the two dukes brothers. In order to strengthen his parallel plots, Shakespeare makes his dukes brothers. He also does not kill the bad duke as in Lodge.

The Forest of Arden, which serves as a retreat from the rat race at court, first for the rightful duke and finally for the usurping Duke Frederick, is the most celebrated of Shakespeare's idealized settings. The Forest of Arden represents nothing less than the simple, unbeguiled past of the human race, itself—a so-called "golden age." It is where Robin Hood, at least according to Arden mythology, dwelled. "Sweet are the uses of adversity," says Duke Senior, after taking in the forest for the first time (2.1.12). From the wrangling at court, he has come to the primitive, mostly innocent, green world of Arden. It is possible that in his portrait of the Forest of Arden, Shakespeare was reliving boyhood memories. His mother's family were Ardens, a shoot of a rich, land-owning family with a forest named after them and with roots going back to pre-Norman times, something that would not have been lost on the poet.[6]

Shakespeare had employed songs in his earliest comedies, but beginning with this comedy, his songs take on a new significance.[7] They relate to the play's theme and to the character of the singer. For example, Amiens has a number of songs throughout the play. He has no real personality, but he can sing and he sings the praises of life in the forest. Typical of the man is the famous song in the second act:

> Under the greenwood tree
> Who loves to lie with me,
> And turn his merry note
> Unto the sweet bird's throat,
> Come hither, come hither, come hither!
> Here shall he see

No enemy
But winter and rough weather. (2.5.1–8)

With *As You Like It*, Shakespeare's acting company, the Lord Chamberlain's Men, worked in a new theater, the Globe, and had a new clown—Robert Armin, known for his singing ability. Will Kempe, the company's principal clown early on, had gone on to other pursuits, most famously a morris dance from London to Norwich, a distance of a hundred miles. The journey took him nine days and immediately afterward, he wrote a book about it. (Just to keep even with the man he replaced, Armin also wrote a number of plays and two jokebooks.)[8]

Robert Armin probably doubled roles in *As You Like It*. His wonderful singing voice would have made him an obvious Amiens, but he probably took on Touchstone as well. As Touchstone, his function is the court jester and he comments derisively on everything he sees, even the Forest of Arden.

Ay, now am I in Arden, the more fool I.
When I was at home, I was in a better place, but
travellers must be content. (2.4.14–16)

Touchstone, as his name shows, is the character in this play, who acts as a tester of the purity, or lack of it, in other characters. But, habitual mocker that he is, Touchstone succumbs to the charms of Audrey and is among the four couples who marry at the play's end.

In *As You Like It*, Shakespeare gives us, perhaps, his most memorable heroine. Her repartee with Orlando in act 3, scene 2, while she is disguised as the youth Ganymede, is a delight.

Love is merely a madness, and, I tell you, deserves as well
a dark horse and a whip as madmen do; and the reason

> why they are not so punished and cured, is that the lunacy is so ordinary that the whippers are in love too.
> (3.2.391–394)

This speech sounds similar to Bottom's observation in *A Midsummer Night's Dream*:

> And yet, to say the truth, reason and love keep little company together nowadays . . . (3.1.137–138)

This idea of equating love and madness crops up as a motif in many of Shakespeare's comedies, early and otherwise. It can be found in *Love's Labour's Lost*, *Much Ado About Nothing*, *A Midsummer Night's Dream*, and *As You Like It*, having such spokespersons as Berowne, Beatrice, Bottom, and Rosalind.

Rosalind is the prime mover of the love matches in this play. She not only hooks Orlando for herself but also brings together Phebe and Silvius and Oliver and Celia. Her exile from the court of Duke Frederick, the usurper, to the Forest of Arden broadens her outlook and deepens her understanding of love. She is fortunate to have a friend in Celia, daughter to the usurping duke, who would rather go into exile with her than live a pampered life at court.

Much Ado About Nothing

In *Much Ado About Nothing*, Shakespeare presents us with his most memorable twosome, Benedick and Beatrice. Though their bickerings make up the subplot of the comedy, they quite overshadow the two leads—Claudio and Hero. Benedick and Beatrice have not been cut from whole cloth by Shakespeare—we have seen them before in Berowne and Rosaline in *Love's Labour's Lost*.

Nevertheless, Benedick and Beatrice are a later, wittier, and more fully developed version of the earlier couple. It is obvious

The Globe Theatre, illustrated here, was built by Shakespeare's company in 1599.

that these two love each other, but, fortunately, they do not choose to show it. Because of this attitude on their part, much of the comedy turns. Disguise and deception are prevalent in the play, which is only natural since true innermost feelings are covered up in the two most memorable characters. This attitude ties in well with a recurring theme of Shakespeare's work—appearance versus reality. As in *Love's Labour's Lost*, there is a great deal of eavesdropping—so much so that the play's name may pack a double meaning—the "Nothing" in the title may be meant to suggest "Noting"—that is, "observing."[9]

Benedick and Beatrice are at odds in their very first meeting (as far as we're concerned—they've met before).

> Beatrice: I wonder that you will still be talking Signior Benedick, nobody marks you.
>
> Benedick: What, my dear Lady Disdain, are you yet living?
>
> Beatrice: Is it possible that disdain should die while she hath such food to feed it as Signior Benedick? Courtesy, itself, must convert to disdain, if you come in her presence.
>
> Benedick: Then is courtesy a turncoat. But it is certain I am lov'd of all ladies, only you excepted; and I would I could find in my heart that I had not a hard heart, for truly I love none.
>
> Beatrice: A dear happiness to women, they would else have been troubled with a pernicious suitor. I thank God and my cold blood, I am of your humor for that. I had rather hear my dog bark at a crow than a man swears he loves me.
>
> Benedick: God keep yor ladyship still in that mind! So some gentleman or other shall scape a predestinate scratch'd face.

> BEATRICE: Scratching could not make it worse, and 'twere such a face as yours were (1.1.112–133)

Much Ado About Nothing ends happily with two marriages. It is reminiscent of *Romeo and Juliet* in that it utilizes a stratagem by a friar to spirit away the heroine until it is safe for her to come out of hiding. In the case of this comedy, the stratagem works.

As usual with Shakespearean comedy, there is mistaken identity—the maid Margaret is taken by Claudio to be his fiancé, Hero. There is also eavesdropping, as we have noted. Both Benedick and Beatrice are made to overhear others tell how much the one loves the other. Shakespeare keeps his

Student actors in Canada perform a scene from *Much Ado About Nothing* in 2007.

characters apart for long intervals so as to stretch out audience anticipation to the fullest. They finally meet after a key turning point. His characters, Claudio and Benedick, most especially, move about the stage as in a fog, while we, the audience, know exactly what's up all the time.

Much Ado is a kissing cousin to *Love's Labour's Lost* but has more refined versions of the earlier comedy's Berowne and Rosalind. Also reminiscent of *Love's Labour's Lost* is the serious note at the end of *Much Ado*. In this case, the sour note concerns the villain, Don John, and his punishment and is the last thing brought up in the comedy. In *Love's Labour's Lost*, the downer is the news of the death of the king of France—but there is yet some two hundred lines to go and room for more fun afterward.

Twelfth Night

Twelfth Night is one of that handful of Shakespeare plays that has a subtitle: *What You Will*. That subtitle, in fact, is the name of a later, wholly unrelated comedy by John Marston, an admirer and imitator of Shakespeare. The idea of a subtitle is interesting because it raises the possibility that the original title of a play or two by Shakespeare got dropped over time and those plays have come down to us by different names. This may have been the case with *Love's Labour's Won*, a comedy by Shakespeare now apparently lost—unless we simply know it by another name.

Shakespeare might just as well have called *Twelfth Night* anything else just as appropriately for all the comedy has to do with Twelfth Night. Twelfth Night, or Epiphany, is the last of the twelve days of Christmas, January 6. The fact that Shakespeare called this Christmas-less play by such a name makes one wonder. The best guess is that this comedy was performed at court for the first time at Epiphany. This time was traditionally one given over to play presentations at court.[10]

Twelfth Night ranks as one of Shakespeare's greatest comedies. The main plot concerns the heroine, Viola, who is involved in a shipwreck off the coast of the mythical Illyria. She fears that her brother, Sebastian, has been drowned. Dressed a boy, she serves the lovelorn Duke Orsino as his page. She falls in love with the duke, but the duke, unaware of who she is and how she feels, uses her to keep in contact with a high-born lady, Olivia. Olivia has vowed not to have anything to do with men for seven years because she wants to spend this time in mourning for her recently deceased brother. But when she sees Viola, dressed as a page and calling herself Cesario, she is smitten. This part of the play is resolved when we find that Sebastian is yet alive and he quickly becomes Olivia's husband. Orsino, discovering the truth about Viola, takes her to be his bride.

The subplot is the really comic portion of the play, with Sir Toby Belch, Olivia's uncle; Sir Andrew Aguecheek, Olivia's suitor; and Fabian, a servant at Olivia's estate, becoming entangled in a broil with Olivia's steward, the pompous Malvolio. This tangle might end in a standoff, were it not for the fact that Malvolio has angered Olivia's clever chambermaid, Maria, who exacts revenge on the steward through a forged letter. The play ends with three happy matches: Viola with Duke Orsino, Olivia with Sebastian, and Maria with Sir Toby.

Twelfth Night, having nothing to do with Christmas, is in league with other inappropriately named Shakespearean comedies—*A Midsummer Night's Dream* and *The Winter's Tale*. As a matter of fact, none of the three great comedies considered here—*As You Like It*, *Much Ado About Nothing*, and *Twelfth Night*—appear to be aptly named. They could have been called most anything else. When we go to a production of *Hamlet* or *Othello*, we have some idea as to what to expect, just from the title. If nothing else, we know that we are dealing with a great tragic hero in these plays. All we can infer from titles like *As You Like It* or *Much Ado* is that we can expect the carefree spirit of comedy.

Danger in the Comedies

It is curious how close Shakespeare comes to tragedy in some of his comedies. Of all his comedies, only *The Taming of the Shrew* does not have a cloud hanging over it. There is never any doubt that all of the characters are going to get out of the five acts alive. This is not the case for the others.

List them and think of their plots. Not one is wholly free of dramatic tension and suspense. Old Aegeon in *The Comedy of Errors* is about to die for being a Syracusan in Ephesus. He has a day to come up with a large ransom or he will be put to death. This sentence hangs over the entire farce of *The Comedy of Errors* and is relieved only in the last scene. In *The Two Gentlemen of Verona*, a deadly duel is anticipated by the audience in the last scene. That it does not take place has been viewed by many as a weakness in the play. Even *A Midsummer Night's Dream*, a comedy in which Shakespeare converts the evil nature of the fairy in folklore to harmless and fun loving, has the threat of death hanging over one of the young heroines.

In *Twelfth Night*, death has been on the premises before the play begins. Olivia, the countess, has lost her brother and she will not entertain any suitors until her time of mourning is past. Viola, in this same play, thinks that her brother has drowned. Again, Antonio, a seafaring man, has enemies in

Illyria and when arrested in act 3, scene 5, he faces death as a former enemy to Orsino, the Duke of Illyria.

The Merchant of Venice, both in its main plot and its romantic subplot, approaches tragedy very closely. Only Portia's letter of the law in not allowing the moneylender Shylock to draw any blood when he takes his pound of flesh from the merchant Antonio prevents his death. Shylock, on the face of it, is the villain of the piece, but he is presented as someone who has been scorned by racial and religious bigotry for being a Jew. He loses his revenge on the merchant, as well as his daughter and jewels. He is not permitted to share in the rejoicing at the play's conclusion. Shakespeare may not have liked Shylock, but he presents his point of view plainly.

The subplot, in which Bassanio has to choose the right casket from three possibilities, is also fraught with unpleasantness. Should Bassanio select the wrong casket, it is all over for him, so far as wedded life is concerned. He chooses correctly and as a result Portia joins him in thwarting Shylock's revenge on Antonio.

The Problem Plays—Comedies That Frown

Three of Shakespeare's plays have been designated by critics as "problem plays." They are *All's Well That Ends Well*, *Measure for Measure*, and *Troilus and Cressida*. One of the common "problems" in each play is the consideration of some social evil—for example, the abuse of authority by the duke's deputy, Angelo, in *Measure For Measure*. Ungoverned lust also crops up in all the problem plays. Our evaluation of these plays depends on how well we think their somewhat contrived endings overcome their shortcomings.

The heroes of these plays are not conventional, nor are they very likable. One might excuse Bertram's behaving like a cad in *All's Well That Ends Well*, but it is difficult to defend Angelo's behavior in *Measure for Measure*. At best he is repentant of his crimes. Troilus is merely misguided and is not to be classed with Angelo and perhaps not with Bertram. As with the comedies, the heroines in these plays, with the exception of Cressida, are to our liking.

All's Well probably comes closest among the problem plays or dark comedies to our conception of comedy. At the play's conclusion, Bertram, the play's hero, is chastened and free of his evil twin, Parolles. He is thus ready to be a good husband, much as in the happier comedies.

Troilus and Cressida was registered to be published in February 1603. No quarto from this time is known. The play had to wait another six years to see print. When it finally did, the printing saw two issues, the second of which bears a colorful address to the "Ever Reader" from the "Never Writer."

Troilus and Cressida is a disturbing play in which nothing is sacred. Love, honor, courage—all are perceived "as through a glass darkly." The two leads are hardly Romeo and Juliet. Cressida is fickle and opportunistic in matters of the heart. Troilus is both a lover and a soldier. He does not see Cressida for the fickle lady that she is. Nor does he see the Trojan War for the dire thing that it is. He sugarcoats both. The play's main outlines have to do with Troilus's love for Cressida. The subplot is built around the Trojan War.

Conclusion

Shakespeare began writing comedy by imitating the Roman farces of Plautus—in *The Comedy of Errors*, he tries his hand at farce and succeeds very well. Immediately thereafter he concerns himself with more character-driven comedies. *Love's*

Right Under Our Noses?

One of Shakespeare's comedies probably has not come down to us. This comedy is *Love's Labour's Won*. It was first mentioned by Francis Meres in his famous list of twelve plays by Shakespeare in his *Palladis Tamia* (1598). By its title, it would appear to be a companion play to *Love's Labour's Lost*. Its mere title suggests a more complete and mirthful comedy than the other, which does not end in a marriage but rather ends in a death (that of the old king of France).

For nearly two centuries after Meres alluded to it, no one took any notice of *Love's Labour's Won*. Finally, when scholars caught on to the fact that at least one of Shakespeare's plays was missing in the 1760s, a belief soon arose that the play is not really missing after all but has simply come down to us under another name. The favorite choice of scholars for the next two centuries was *All's Well That Ends Well*. This dark comedy shows two distinct metrical styles—one early, one late. The conclusion of scholars was that *All's Well* is the name of the revision Shakespeare made of *Love's Labour's Won* at some point near the beginning of the seventeenth century.

In 1953, an inventory turned up at the back of a book of old sermons that showed that *Love's Labour's Won* had been published by 1603. In the past half century, other Shakespearean plays have been put forth as an alternately titled *Love's Labour's Won*—but none have been as convincing as the idea that the play was simply lost.[12]

Even so, one cannot wholly escape the notion that pieces of the play can be found in such poetic miscellanies as *The Passionate Pilgrim* and *England's Helicon*.

Labour's Lost, written early in his career, showcases his growth. He used no source for this play—just his own imagination.

Shakespeare wrote his plays according to the fashion then current, but he periodically tended to indulge his whimsy. He seems to have taken up *Love's Labour's Lost*, for example, to make fun of somebody that needed mocking. Or possibly he was reflecting on people he knew growing up in Warwickshire. In any case, the humor seems sardonic and well aimed. *A Midsummer Night's Dream* must have been written for a performance alongside a wedding—we do not know for whom. Later he would write *The Merry Wives of Windsor*, possibly as a favor to Queen Elizabeth. Again, there is no major source for this play—he is just out having fun, at the expense of the German Count Mompelgard, for one.[11]

Shakespeare reaches his peak of comedy with the golden, or mature, comedies: *Much Ado About Nothing*, *As You Like It*, and *Twelfth Night*. No sooner has he done so, however, than once again he begins to explore a type of comedy that borders on tragedy right up to the moment of its resolution (the problem plays). They take up sexual mores and class distinctions and the nature of a good ruler. The endings to these plays leave much up in the air and seem more contrived than logical in their outcomes.

Shakespeare Hits His Stride: *A Midsummer Night's Dream*

Essayist and caricaturist Sir Max Beerbohm once said of *A Midsummer Night's Dream*: "Here we have the Master, confident in his art, at ease with it as a man in his dressing gown, kicking up a loose slipper and catching it on his toe."[1] But two centuries earlier, the diarist, Samuel Pepys (pronounced Peeps) found the play "the most insipid ridiculous comedy that ever I saw." That was the Restoration for you—they were always trying to improve on Shakespeare!

By 1595, Shakespeare pretty much knew what he was doing when it came to comedy. The simplistic ending of *The Two Gentlemen of Verona* was behind him for all time. The easy laughs of the farcical *The Comedy of Errors* would also be absent from this new comedy. Shakespeare was ready to get back to that world first broached in *The Two Gentlemen of Verona*—a green world in which a good part of the action takes place in the woods. He also knew how to slip in a song—no easy task in so lyrical a play as *A Midsummer Night's Dream*.

Full of mischief as this comedy is, and full of the plights and pitfalls of young love (a sort of comical *Romeo and Juliet*), it has always been one of Shakespeare's most popular plays. The clowns, or "rude mechanicals," as they are known in this comedy, led by Nick Bottom, have always made the play, and their nonsense in the decades following Shakespeare's death in 1616 was taken out and performed separately.[2]

An illustration depicts Bottom (with the ass's head) and Titania in a scene from *A Midsummer Night's Dream*.

Shakespeare probably wrote *A Midsummer Night's Dream* around 1595 (though earlier and later dates have been proposed). It is mentioned by Francis Meres in 1598 and was published two years later as a quarto. Its lyrical style and concern with young love recalls *Romeo and Juliet*.

Characterization

A Midsummer Night's Dream contains Shakespeare's most memorable clown up to this point in his career. In Nick Bottom, the overly enthusiastic actor, who would play both Pyramus and Thisby, Shakespeare crafted his most entertaining funnyman until Falstaff's appearance in *1 Henry IV*. We know little about Bottom—whether he's married and has children or if he's ever been in love, even—something we might wish to know in a comedy like this. He is before us, speaking prose and misapplying it with abandon. For instance, he quotes the Bible in the first scene of act 4 (209–211), only to get it wrong. (The passage concerned is 1 Corinthians 2:9.) Only Nick Bottom could say something like this:

> I have an exposition of sleep come upon me. (4.1.38)

In fact, he means "disposition," or inclination to sleep.

When Puck's mischief results in his having an ass's head, he becomes a figure of fun but also one for whom we can feel. He is isolated from his fellow artisans, who run from him and can have no idea that in another moment the beautiful Queen of the Fairies will be in love with him. Of course, Bottom can get used to this new situation readily, even as he can eat hay owing to his having an ass's head.

> Good hay, sweet hay, hath no fellow. (4.1.33)

Bottom, like the young lovers, will awaken without the ass's head and will wonder if he has been dreaming, just as the young people do.

Hermia and Helena, like their male counterparts, Lysander and Demetrius, are not carefully drawn. Shakespeare does not want us to be overly concerned about them. They are four posts to hang a plot on. In this play, Shakespeare is concerned with comic misadventures more than those characters caught up in them.

Theseus is a figure of law and order and, as such, someone necessary to any Shakespearean play. He overrules the harsh measure that Egeus would impose on his daughter, Hermia, so that the play can end happily. Hippolyta, after the comedy begins, is of one accord with her husband and is pretty much a spectator to the story, or rather, commentator, for she has wit, as seen in her elaboration of an observation made by her husband (5.1.211–212). She is no cookie-cutter, stock character. Shakespeare introduces Theseus and Hippolyta in differing verse patterns in their first speeches.

The imperious Theseus, thinking of his wedding date, speaks lines whose sense is not end-stopped but runs over into the next line, thereby conveying his anticipation of his nuptials. Hippolyta, conversely, replies with two lines of end-stopped blank verse. We thus get the feeling that two different people are talking.

> Theseus: Now, fair Hippolyta, our nuptial hour
> Draws on apace. Four happy days bring in
> Another moon; but O, methinks, how slow
> This old moon wanes! She lingers my desires,
> Like to a step-dame, or a dowager,
> Long withering out a young man's revenue.

> HIPPOLYTA: Four days will quickly steep themselves in night;
> Four nights will quickly dream away the time;
> And then the moon, like to a silver bow
> New bent in heaven, shall behold the night
> Of our solemnities. (1.1.1–11)

Oberon and Titania are typical fairies out of the folklore of that day, albeit tempered by Shakespeare's good humor. Otherwise they might have worked black magic on these mortals in love. The same is true of Oberon's trusty minion, Puck. Puck sums up human activity after getting a good look at it in the form of the lovers in the forest and especially Nick Bottom:

> Lord, what fools these mortals be! (3.2.115)

Only one character in this play grates on our modern sensibilities. The notion of a father demanding unconditional obedience from his daughter in a matter of the heart is quite alien to our values. Ideally, women, even terribly young ones, have the right to pick their boyfriends. But in *A Midsummer Night's Dream*, Egeus will have nothing of his daughter's attraction for Lysander. His choice, as one might not expect, falls on Demetrius—a "love 'em and leave 'em" type. Such wrong-mindedness in a father closely parallels Old Capulet's handling of his daughter Juliet's engagement to Paris in *Romeo and Juliet*. It introduces the one really disquieting element in this comedy. People like Egeus, who cling to their views without regard to what is right, often kill the thing they love. Egeus's pigheadedness can kill his daughter outright or, at the very least, kill her desire for life.

end-stopped

A line of poetry that is a complete sentence (i.e., when one line does not continue into the next line).

If *Romeo and Juliet* comes up often in discussing *A Midsummer Night's Dream*, there are reasons enough for it. Both plays were mentioned by Francis Meres in 1598, so they both must have been written by that time and, in fact, *Romeo and Juliet* was published in a corrupt quarto by then. Fate is mentioned by Hermia early in *A Midsummer Night's Dream*:

> If then true lovers have been ever cross'd,
> It stands as an edict in destiny. (1.1.150–151)

It is likewise mentioned in the famous Prologue to *Romeo and Juliet*:

> A pair of star-cross'd lovers take their life;
> Whose misadventur'd piteous overthrows
> Doth with their death bury their parents' strife. (Prol. 6–8)

Lysander, in this play, speaks of "lightning in the collied night" (1.1.145), which has its counterpart in Juliet's "Too like the lightning, which doth cease to be/Ere one can say, 'It lightens'" (2.2.119–120).

Both plays employ dream imagery—*A Midsummer Night's Dream* (1.1.144) and *Romeo and Juliet* (2.2.140). The two plays share a common theme too, which is found in Lysander's observation that "the course of true love never did run smooth" (1.1.134).

Style

Notice that, outside of his role as Pyramus in the interlude, Bottom speaks prose. All of Shakespeare's rustics speak in prose. Shakespeare operated on the caste system. If a character wants to speak in verse, that character had better be highborn or, at the very least, have the decency to talk to someone highborn.

It is interesting that the young lovers in this play are hardly distinguishable.[3] Hermia is short and dark and Helena tall and blonde, but it matters little. They could be any of us. Love is the result of a magical juice squeezed out of a "little western flower" (pansy) on their eyes or our own.

A Midsummer Night's Dream is one of Shakespeare's most lyrical plays. It is only exceeded in rhyme by one of his least popular plays—*Love's Labour's Lost*.[4] It has a fair amount of prose mixed in. About one-sixth of the play is prose.[5] This is the result of the appearances by Bottom and the other craftsmen. Puck and the fairies, including Oberon, sprinkle songs throughout the proceedings, though, as yet, these songs do not generate the theme of the play as they do in the later more mature comedies.[6] They are incidental—a commentary on things in passing.

Spectators enjoy a performance of *A Midsummer Night's Dream* at the Globe Theatre in 2013.

A Midsummer Night's Dream is a highly structured play. The action goes from the court (Athens) to the woods and back again. The artisans have two appearances before Bottom's transformation into a man with an ass's head and twice afterward. A song is sung when Titania is put to sleep with a potion and again when she is awakened from the effects of the drug. Within the space of a few lines, both sets of lovers relate that they have awakened from a dream. This experience is echoed by Bottom a few lines later. His ironic take on all this is as follows:

> Man is but an ass, if he go about to expound this dream. Methought I was—and methought I had—but man is but a patched fool if he will offer to say what he methought I had. The eye of man hath not heard, the ear of man hath not seen, man's hand is not able to taste, his tongue to conceive, nor his heart to report, what my dream was. (4.1.205–212)

Shakespeare closes the play with an *epithalamium*, or wedding song, spoken by Oberon (5.1.395–416). Probably the most notable epithalamium in Elizabethan literature is Spenser's *Epithalamion*, celebrating the poet's marriage to Elizabeth Boyle, published in 1595. That Shakespeare uses an epithalamium in this play suggests its purpose in celebrating a real-life wedding, possibly that of someone present at the play and for whom it was presented.

allegorical

Relating to allegory; when something is designed to represent or symbolize something else.

Such a thing relates this play to the masque, a courtly entertainment, full of elaborate costumes and music and dancing. The characters in it are mythological or allegorical figures. The probable allusion in the second act to Queen Elizabeth as "the imperial vot'ress . . . /In maiden meditation, fancy-free," perhaps signifies a performance of this play at Court or for her benefit, at least (2.1.158–164). Whomsoever this play was written for must have been important, indeed, since the queen most likely was present when it was first presented.

Bottom's Dream

Is this play a dream or reality? Bottom has an inspiration to call his transformation "Bottom's Dream." Theseus dismisses the fantastic experiences of the two young couples as a dream:

> More strange than true. I never may believe
> These antic fables, nor these fairy toys.
> Lovers and madmen have such seething brains,
> Such shaping fantasies, that apprehend
> More than cool reason ever comprehends.
> The lunatic, the lover, and the poet,
> Are imagination all compact. (5.1.2–8)

Is there, when all is said and done, any difference between love and lunacy? In the end, it is Puck who has the last word. He gives the audience a choice to believe what they please, dream or otherwise.

> If we shadows have offended,
> Think but this and all is mended,
> That you have but slumbered here
> While these visions did appear.
> And this weak and idle theme,
> No more yielding but a dream. (5.1.417–422)

This is interesting coming from Puck, who is precisely one of those creatures that we meet only in a dream—or our worst nightmare.

"FIND OUT MOONSHINE!"

In the first scene of act 3 in *A Midsummer Night's Dream*, Bottom shouts, "A calendar, a calendar! Look in the almanac; find out moonshine, find out moonshine!"

One can imagine Abraham Lincoln, as a lawyer confronted with his most famous case, saying very nearly the same words. In May 1858, Lincoln defended a young man charged with murder. The prosecution's chief witness claimed to have seen the killing when the moon was about the height that the sun is at ten in the morning. Lincoln called for an almanac and found that at the night in question, there was a new moon that could not have been so high as the witness claimed.

"Who dreamed that Beauty passes like a dream?" William Butler Yeats wondered.[7] It may be that we all do. Certainly, Shakespeare did.

Themes and Parallels

Lysander states the theme of the comedy when he says:

> The course of true love never did run smooth. (1.1.134)

The theme of *A Midsummer Night's Dream*, like that of *Romeo and Juliet*, is that love is unpredictable and, for all its charm, not that easy to deal with. This goes for young people like Romeo and Juliet but also for more seasoned ones like Theseus and Hippolyta (judging by their past). Even the fairies, Oberon and Titania, are prey to love's spell. Only the rustics have no history connected with love. We do not know whether Bottom or Peter Quince has a wife and kids or even a cat to keep him company. Yet they too are caught up in the romantic goings-on in the play. They will enact an interlude called *Pyramus and Thisby*, written by Quince. This Peter Quince, by the way, must be quite a hand at passionate writing, for when Bottom awakens from his dream, he immediately thinks of having Quince write a prologue about it. Quince at least knows what a prologue of "eight and six" looks like (3.1. 21–22). Is Quince thinking of *Romeo and Juliet*? The fact that Quince suggests a second prologue is an example of an oxymoron, as how can there be two prologues back to back?

Hermia and Lysander, but for a kindly and beneficent fate, could have been Romeo and Juliet. Fate is always just around the corner in this play, as in the tragedy, and lives and loves hang in the balance in both plays. It is easy to believe that Shakespeare wrote the one with his right hand while writing the other with his left. Indeed, one is led to the inescapable conviction that Shakespeare wrote *A Midsummer Night's Dream* and *Romeo and Juliet* back to back, just as (most probably) *Love's Labour's Lost* and the missing *Love's Labour's Won* were.

Early on, Hermia and Lysander discuss love. They both have been discussing love stories. They could well have been thinking of Pyramus and Thisby, the subject of the interlude given by the rustics at the play's conclusion. But it almost sounds as though they have been reading about Romeo and Juliet.

> LYSANDER: Ay me! for aught that I could ever read,
> Could ever hear by tale or history,
> The course of true love never did run smooth;
> But either it was different in blood—
> HERMIA: O cross! too high to be enthrall'd to [low]
> LYSANDER: Or else misgraffed in respect of years—
> HERMIA: O spite! too old to be engag'd to young.

Lysander: Or, if there were a sympathy in choice,
War, death, or sickness did lay siege to it,
Making it momentary as sound,
Swift as a shadow, short as any dream,
Brief as the lightning in the collied night,
That in a spleen, unfolds both heaven and earth,
And ere a man hath power to say, "Behold!"
The jaws of darkness do devour it up:
So quick bright things come to confusion.
Hermia: If then true lovers have been ever cross'd,
It stands as an edict in destiny.
Then let us teach each other patience,
Because it is a customary cross,
As due to love as thoughts and dreams as sighs,
Wishes and tears, poor fancy's followers. (1.1.132–155)

Symbols

Due to the lack of scenery in the public theaters in which this comedy was staged, Shakespeare has to use highly descriptive figures of speech to set his scenes. The result is that his language in this play is highly figurative. As we might expect, the moon and moonlight are often brought up in the play. The moon conveys a strong hint of the lunacy that affects madmen and lovers, especially in the heat of midsummer (even though this play takes place in early May.) One character in the interlude is even named Moonshine. But the moon conveys the constancy of love as well. Lovers cannot pledge their troths without swearing by the moon.

The sense of dreaming is furthermore enhanced by all the play's allusions to the moon (more than any of Shakespeare's other plays, though this figure must take into account that one of the players in the interlude is named "Moonshine" and is addressed as such.) Also, logically enough for a play largely set

Quince's Interlude

The story of Pyramus and Thisby (or "Thisbe") comes from Ovid and was familiar to members of Shakespeare's audience. It tells of two young lovers who are kept apart by a wall. One night when they are to rendezvous, a lion scares Thisby away. She leaves a piece of her clothing behind as she flees and the curious lion, having just eaten, gets blood on the item. Pyramus happens along and sees the bloodied clothing and assumes the worst. Believing Thisby was eaten by the lion, he kills himself. Thisby returns, sees the lifeless form of Pyramus, and likewise kills herself.

in the woods, many of the images deal with plants and flowers as well as animals.

The two settings found in this play may be taken as symbols, too. The court of Duke Theseus, in which the play begins and ends, is representative of order, just as Theseus is the epitome of reason. The woods, on the other hand, are the domain of the fairies and, as such, anything but tame and orderly. In these brakes and streams outside of Athens, anything can happen. If only the lovers had stayed in Athens, none of these adventures would have followed—but then the play would not end happily.

Literary Devices in *A Midsummer Night's Dream*

Hyperbole and Puns

Bottom is supremely confident in his ignorance of most things. This makes him naturally prone to exaggerate, the essence of hyperbole. So it is with acting, about which he knows nothing. When the interlude is sketched for him, he says:

> I will move storms; I will condole in some measure. To the rest—Yet my chief humor is for a tyrant. I could play Ercles rarely, or a part to tear a cat in, to make all split . . . (1.2.24–27)

Bottom also makes liberal use of puns:

> if that you should fright the ladies out of their wits, they would have no more discretion but to hang us. (1.2.75–77)
>
> In this instance, "wits" means both "mind" and "judgment." Later on (5.1.307–308, 310–311), "die," meaning death, stands for "die," meaning one of a pair of dice. "Ace," again referring to dice, is punned with "ass." And Helena puns on hail/hale.
>
> He hailed down oaths that he was only mine;
>
> And when this hail some heat from Hermia felt,
>
> So he dissolv'd and show'rs of oaths did melt— (1.1.243–45)

Oxymorons

Oxymorons set down two opposites in close association. The play within this play, *Pyramus and Thisby*, either makes use of oxymorons or inspires them. In act 5, we have this description of the interlude, read by Theseus and wondered at by him:

> "A tedious brief scene of young Pyramus
> And his love Thisby; a very tragical mirth."
>
> Merry and tragical! tedious and brief!
> That is, hot ice and wondrous strange snow.
> How shall we find the concord of this discord? (5.1.56–60)

Similes

A simile compares two things and is easily identified by the words "as" or "like." Theseus no sooner opens his mouth in the play than a simile comes out. Referring to the moon, he says:

> She lingers my desires,
> Like to a step-dame, or a dowager,
> Long withering out a young man's revenue. (1.1.4–6)

Personification

Personification attributes living characteristics to inanimate objects or abstractions. Theseus personifies mirth and melancholy:

> Awake the pert and nimble spirit of mirth,
> Turn melancholy forth to funerals:
> The pale companion is not for our pomp. (1.1.13–15)

Later in the play, at the height of the quarrel between the King and Queen of Fairies, Titania says:

> and the green corn
> Hath rotted ere his youth attain'd a beard. (2.1.94–95)

Alliteration

Alliteration is the repetition of words beginning with the same consonant. In this play, Shakespeare parodies the high-flown language of some earlier dramatists with alliterative passages in *Pyramus* and *Thisby*. Thus:

> He bravely broach'd his boiling bloody breast; (5.1.146)

Also:

> For by thy gracious, golden, glittering [gleams]. (5.1.268)

7

Romeo and Juliet: The Last Word on First Love

We can't say for sure when Shakespeare wrote *Romeo and Juliet*. Because of an earthquake mentioned by Juliet's nurse (1.3.23), a date as early as 1591 has been proposed. But stylistic evidence makes a date of 1595 or 1596 almost certain. In any case, the play was in print by 1597.

Nothing by Shakespeare has been more beloved by audiences and readers alike as *Romeo and Juliet*. Both old and young are fascinated by the all-consuming passion of the two Veronese teens whose names have come to symbolize youthful love and true devotion. The play enjoyed more major film productions in the last century, more than even *Hamlet* and *Macbeth* have received.[1] *Romeo and Juliet* remains remarkably fresh and relevant to every generation.

Not that the story of Romeo and Juliet was Shakespeare's invention. Indeed, in Shakespeare's time, the story of the ill-fated young lovers was considered historical. Italian novellas told the story in its basic outlines. After one novella by Bandello had been translated in French in 1556, the English poet Arthur Brooke came to it and shaped it into a long narrative poem called *The Tragical Historye of Romeus and Juliet* (1562). Brooke had an ax to grind and it was wielded at Romeo and Juliet, in particular, for their rash love and disobedience—to their parents, specifically, and at Roman Catholicism in

An artist's rendering of the dramatic final scene of *Romeo and Juliet.*

general. Needless to say, Shakespeare softened the Puritanical tone of his source.

When Shakespeare came to the story of Romeo and Juliet, he had previously written only one tragedy. This was the so-called "tragedy of blood," *Titus Andronicus*. This type of play was in demand at the time, much like the "slasher" films of recent years. Perhaps because of this, *Titus* is not memorable Shakespeare.

Shakespeare was to work very differently in *Romeo and Juliet*. Whereas *Titus Andronicus* was almost inexhaustible in its gore, *Romeo and Juliet*, in its first two acts, could nearly pass for a comedy. Its outcome, however, would lead to plenty of corpses—six or seven, depending on which version of the play is used, compared to eleven in his first effort.[2]

The Poetry of *Romeo and Juliet*

In *Romeo and Juliet*, Shakespeare was displaying a virtuosity and brilliance unlooked for from readers and spectators of his earlier tragedy. This is probably because *Titus* is an early work, possibly pre-dating his poems *Venus and Adonis* and *The Rape of Lucrece* and, most probably, the sonnets. *Romeo and Juliet* followed his poems immediately or may even have been written right alongside of them.[3]

A Midsummer Night's Dream reveals a Shakespeare sure of himself in handling comedy in a lyrical vein. *Romeo and Juliet* does the same for Shakespearean tragedy. One notes a great variety of verse forms in this tragedy. There are rhymed couplets—used by Shakespeare at all points in his career as a sort of curtain puller to end a scene. There are four-line quatrains and six-line sestets and eight-line octets and even whole sonnets of fourteen lines. As Arthur Brooke in his *Romeus and Juliet* had led things off with a summarizing sonnet, so Shakespeare leads *Romeo and Juliet* off with a prologue made up of a single sonnet. Later, a sonnet also leads off the second act of the tragedy.

But most remarkably, Shakespeare envelops the first meeting of the two young lovers in a sonnet. One has only to look at these lines to see that not only do they demand a certain rhythm but a varying volume as well. We can almost hear them on the printed page.

> ROMEO: If I profane with my unworthiest hand *a*
> This holy shrine, the gentle fine is this, *b*
> My lips, two blushing pilgrims ready stand *a*
> To smooth that rough touch with a tender kiss. *b*
> JULIET: Good pilgrim, you do wrong your hand too much, *c*
> Which mannerly devotion shows in this, *b*
> For saints have hands that pilgrims' hands do touch, *c*
> And palm to palm is holy palmers' kiss. *b*
> ROMEO: Have not saints lips, and holy palmers to? *d*
> JULIET: Ay, pilgrim, lips that they must use in prayer. *e*
> ROMEO: O, then, dear saint, let lips do what hands do! *d*
> They pray; grant thou, lest faith turn to despair. *e*
> JULIET: Saints do move, though grant for prayers' sake. *f*
> ROMEO: Then move not while my prayer's effect I take. *f*
> (1.5.93–106)

This sonnet moves the play along at a key point, the first such in the play. It is also a charming moment, as indeed it should be. It is the first meeting of Romeo and Juliet and the sonnet is fourteen lines of love at first sight. Each of the fourteen lines is in iambic pentameter, meaning that there are five feet of alternately stressed and unstressed beats. The rhyme scheme, however, is a bit unusual—ababcbcbdedeff—instead of Shakespeare's usual octave of ababcdcd and sestet of efefgg.

Shakespeare was employing sonnets in other plays that were written at this time—*Love's Labour's Lost*, *The Merchant of Venice*, and *A Midsummer Night's Dream*. Many of the speeches in *Romeo and Juliet* are sonnets—or octaves and sestets, those building blocks of sonnets—right down to the final six lines of the play. Sonnets can be about anything they please, but usually they trade in love. When Shakespeare wrote *Romeo and Juliet*, there were a number of sonnet sequences in the air and he at least began, if not completed, his own cycle of sonnets at this time.

Another instance of Shakespeare's poetic skill in this play comes in act 4. Old Capulet is preparing for Juliet's upcoming wedding to Paris and cries out:

> Nurse! Wife! What, ho! What, nurse, I say! (4.4.23)

The line appears to be non-metrical at first glance, just plain prose. Yet it keeps pace with the march of iambic pentameter by quietly devoting an unstressed syllabic pause in front of the words, "Nurse" and "Wife."[4] The line is poetic because, nearly always, Shakespeare's highborn characters speak in verse. Menials, rustics, and clowns always steep themselves in prose. Juliet's nurse, however, is so delighted by Shakespeare that she often speaks iambic pentameter, quite unlike other common folk.

The poetic highpoint of the play arrives in the famous balcony scene where Romeo woos Juliet. (These lines were worn out by students at Oxford University where an old Folio was chained to a desk for their benefit.[5]) Romeo has met Juliet at the Capulet ball in the last scene of the first act, at which point he quickly forgets about Rosaline. For her part, Juliet is taken with Romeo upon sight:

O gentle Romeo,
If thou dost love, pronounce it faithfully.
Or if thou thinkest I am too quickly won,
I'll frown and be perverse and say thee nay,
So thou wilt woo; but else, not for the world,
In truth, fair Montague, I am too fond
And therefore thou mayst think my behavior light.
But trust me, gentleman, I'll prove more true
Than those that have more coying to be strange.
I should have been more strange, I must confess,
But that thou overheard'st, ere I was ware,
My true-love passion. Therefore pardon me,
And not impute this yielding to light love,
Which the dark night hath so discovered. (2.2.93–106)

Romeo and Juliet is well above Shakespeare's average when it comes to the use of blank verse, with 2,111 of its nearly 3,000 lines total being blank verse. The prose in *Romeo and Juliet* is limited to 405 lines, something less than average, even for an early play.[6] Prose finds its way into the play right off with the quarreling minions in the first scene.

The nurse, whose lowly station in life would lead one to think that she should speak prose all the time, does not. Around Romeo, she speaks verse at first, then prose when she encounters him with Mercutio.

Characters

Tybalt

But for one character, *Romeo and Juliet* would have a happy ending. That character is Tybalt. He is the serpent in the garden. His type crops up again and again in Shakespeare's plays. Aaron in *Titus Andronicus*, Don John in *Much Ado About Nothing*, Iago in *Othello*, and Cloten in *Cymbeline* are all his kith and kin. These people are all completely evil, though at least Tybalt has Juliet and her mother's affection—probably owing to nothing more than blood ties. The fact that Tybalt goes on hating when everyone else is ready to make up lies at the heart of this tragedy. Tybalt is utterly without humor—so is the prince, but then he is busy keeping order all the time—and when Old Capulet gives him his cue for fair play and accommodation at the ball in act 1, scene 5, he will have none of it. Tybalt will not learn from example or precept. His hand is ever on his sword.

In reviewing the Johnston Forbes-Robertson production of *Romeo and Juliet* in September 1895, George Bernard Shaw had this to say of Tybalt: "Tybalt's is such an unmercifully bad part that one can hardly demand anything from its representative except that he should brush his hair when he comes to his uncle's ball . . . and that he should be so consummate a swordsman as to make it safe for Romeo to fall on him with absolute abandonment, and annihilate him."[7]

Romeo

When we first encounter Romeo, we see him as head over heels in love—but not with Juliet. He is in love with the "fair Rosaline," but she does not return his affection. This is apparent from the way Romeo carries on about it with Benvolio. In this first glimpse we have of him, it appears clear that Romeo is one of those characters dear to Shakespeare's heart—someone who is in love with love.

Once Romeo meets Juliet, things change for him. He is consumed by his passion for her. He is no longer an adolescent in the throes of puppy love. He is experiencing the real thing to such a degree that he marries Juliet the day after meeting her. As we have seen, the love between Romeo and Juliet takes on an almost religious quality. This is obvious from the language of the sonnet describing the first meeting of the two, which includes words like "pilgrim," "profane," "saints," "holy palmers," and "prayer."

In his encounter with Tybalt in the pivotal scene of the play in act 3, scene 1, Romeo is as mature as he shall ever get. Tybalt prods him, and Romeo turns the other cheek, owing to the fact that he has just married Juliet, Tybalt's cousin. Romeo now is all grown up. Of course, when Juliet is taken out of the equation, he is not to be trusted to use good judgment. He becomes rash, rushing back to Verona from Mantua, then killing Paris at Juliet's tomb. Had he done neither of these things, Romeo and Juliet might have survived all five acts.

Juliet

Juliet, too, changes over the course of the play. She goes from a demure, sweet little girl, embarrassed by the nurse's nonsense and perfect in her obedience to her parents, to a headstrong, very focused young woman, who, save for Romeo's love, is all alone in this world. She divorces herself from her parents and her surrogate parent, the nurse, at the end of the third act. She will yet have Friar Lawrence as a confidant and her contact with Romeo, but from the beginning of act 4, she is pretty much alone with her thoughts.

Apart from Mercutio's inimitable Queen Mab confection, the most lyrical speeches in the play are hers.

> Gallop apace, you fiery-footed steeds,
> Towards Phoebus' lodging; such a waggoner
> As Phaeton would whip you to the west,
> And bring in cloudy night immediately,
> Spread thy close curtain, love-perfuming night,
> That the runaway's eyes may wink, and Romeo

Leap to these arms untalk'd of and unseen!
Lovers can see to do their amorous rites
By their own beauties, or, if love be blind,
It best agrees with night. Come, civil night,
Thou sober-suited matron, all in black,
And learn me how to lose a winning match,
Play'd for a pair of stainless maidenhoods. (3.2.1–13)

Juliet is not only lyrical but, quite unlike her cousin, Tybalt, she has a marvelous sense of humor. In this, she is like the madcap Mercutio, Romeo's friend, and, indeed, like Romeo himself. In fact, Juliet has the best two gags in the play. When the nurse takes her sweet time telling "little Jule" what has transpired with Romeo and will not come to the point (somewhat on purpose because it is fun to torment the girl), she begins with her aching joints. Juliet rounds on her thus:

I would thou hadst my bones, and I thy news. (2.5.27)

When the nurse mentions that she is out of breath, Juliet replies:

How art thou out of breath, when thou hast breath
To say to me that thou art out of breath? (2.5.31–32)

This exchange comes just before the pivotal scene in the opening scene of act 3, in which Juliet will lose Tybalt, her kinsman, and Romeo loses his friend Mercutio. It depicts Shakespeare's way of relieving tension at key points in his dramas and keeps us guessing as to the play's outcome.

Friar Lawrence

On the whole, we see more of Juliet with her family than we do Romeo with his. In fact, on stage Romeo does not share one scene with his father (or mother). This may be intended to make Friar Lawrence his father figure, because the friar has things to do in the play. Much that goes wrong would not go wrong if it were not for Friar Lawrence, well-meaning man that he is. On the other hand, Old Montague is around only at the beginning and at the end of the play and ever so briefly in the critical action of the opening scene of the third act.

Other Characters

Lesser figures in the play are still fully developed. Mercutio, Romeo's friend, is a foil to Romeo. His views on love are cynical, not romantic like Romeo's. His death, owing to Romeo's intention to make peace between the two feuding families, is the turning point of the tragedy. So long as Mercutio lived, Romeo is under his lighthearted spell. Up to his death, audiences might even have wondered whether they had walked in on a comedy. The famous "Queen Mab" speech (1.4.53–94) proclaims Mercutio one of Shakespeare's poets, but his goading of Tybalt (3.1) reveals his volatile, out-of-control nature. His very name, Mercutio, resembles the word *mercurial*, suggesting volatility and extremes of temperament. Mercutio is a gladiator in a clown's clothing.

The nurse is as bawdy as a woman gets in Shakespeare. In this, she keeps pace with Mercutio (which takes some doing), preferring to be racy right up to her final word in Juliet's ear (4.5.11). There is a place for her in our affection when we think that things may turn out all right, but after Juliet dismisses her as "Ancient damnation" (3.5.235), there is less charm in her rough edges.

Capulet, too, has his points. We love him for putting Tybalt in his place in no uncertain terms at the ball (1.5.82–88), but his impetuous way with Juliet cools our admiration of him. As the head of a household in a patriarchal society, we can perhaps understand where he is coming from, but as the father of such a daughter, we have to wonder what he is thinking. He makes no attempt to see things from Juliet's point of view. Instead, he merely dictates his will to her. And it is his will that Juliet marry Paris. Again, were it not for the momentous scene in the opening of the third act, he might not have been so imperious regarding her marriage to Paris. But killing Tybalt has made Romeo an unacceptable choice for Juliet and it is not possible for Capulet to be the accepting, patient man that we find him when Paris first asks for Juliet's hand.

foil

A character who is nearly the direct opposite of the hero or heroine of a story.

Literary Devices in *Romeo and Juliet*

Personification

There is a good bit of personification when Romeo says of the unconscious Juliet:

> Death that hath suck'd the honey of thy breath,
> Hath had no power yet upon thy beauty; (5.3.92–93)

Earlier Friar Lawrence gives us this gem of personification:

> The grey-ey'd morn smiles on the frowning night,
> Check'ring the eastern clouds with streaks of light,
> And fleckled darkness like a drunkard reels
> From forth day's path and Titan's fiery wheels. (2.3.1–4)

These figurative lines, by the way, come on the heels of the balcony scene, probably the most breathtakingly lyrical composition in literature—a tough act to follow. But Friar Lawrence, in these lines, keeps up the high standards of Shakespeare's verse.

In act 3, Juliet says:

Mercutio

Mercutio steals the show whenever he's on. Watch any production of *Romeo and Juliet* and you'll see how hard it is to contain him, verbally and physically. The poet/dramatist/critic John Dryden, in an essay written a half-century after Shakespeare's death, tells how someone asked Shakespeare why he killed Mercutio off in the third act. Shakespeare replied that he had to—it was either him or me.

> Come, gentle night; come, loving black-browed night . . .
> (3.2.20)

Later in the same act, Romeo takes his sad leave of his new wife, saying:

> Night's candles are burnt out, and jocund day
> Stands tiptoe on the mountain tops. (3.5.9–10)

From these examples of personification, we can see yet another means whereby Shakespeare unites these two personalities. Time, in the form of day and night, has a living significance for them. This arises from Shakespeare compressing the timespan in his sources.

Oxymorons

The lovelorn Romeo, when we first encounter him, quite bereft of his Rosaline, sprinkles his speech liberally with oxymorons.

It apparently releases pent-up pressure in him, not only for his sake but for his family's. Coming upon the scene of the fray between the retainers of his Montague faction and the Capulets, Romeo cries:

O heavy lightness, serious vanity,
Misshapen chaos of well-seeming forms,
Feather of lead, bright smoke, cold fire, sick health,
Still-waking sleep that is not what it is! (1.1.178–181)

There is much in these few lines to ponder in terms of Shakespeare's outlook. "Sick-health" conjures up his preoccupation with disease imagery in this play and others such as *Hamlet*. "Still-waking sleep" puts us in mind of the many insomniacs in his plays, usually monarchs but also Lady Macbeth, who envy those of us who do not wear a crown or own a bad conscience. The last part of the second line, "that is not what it is," recalls the appearance-versus-reality theme that is a constant in Shakespeare.

Puns and Quibbles

In the first act, Montague speaks of Romeo thus:

Away from light steals home my heavy son. (1.1.137)

Here, we find a play on "light" in the sense of sunlight as a noun as well as lightweight as an adjective. Romeo may not have a single scene with his father, but from such wordplay—light/heavy—we can see that he is his father's son.

Later on, Juliet says:

Or those eyes shut, that make thee answer,
"Ay" . . . (3.2.49)

Besides giving editors grief over the years in trying to decide whether Shakespeare meant "shut" or "shot" (the reading of the Second Quarto), the line puns on eye/ay. In fact, this line is part of an extended play over several lines on three words with the same sound: "I," "ay," and "eye."

No discussion of puns in *Romeo and Juliet* can afford to overlook Mercutio's pun when he is already a dead man. After receiving a mortal wound from Tybalt, due to Romeo's intervention, he says (in prose): "Ask for me tomorrow, and you shall find me a grave man." (3.1.98–99)

Metaphor and Simile

When Romeo asks her what he should swear by, Juliet says:

> Swear by thy gracious self . . . the god of my idolatry. (2.2.113–114)

Juliet's reply is a metaphor, turning Romeo into an object of religious devotion.

Similes are comparisons that employ the telltale "like" or "as" that alert us to their presence. Mercutio has a long-winded simile dealing with Benvolio's supposedly short fuse (3.1.5–9). Juliet compares Romeo to a bird with thread tied to his leg:

> Like a poor prisoner in his twisted gyves. (2.2.179)

Foreshadowing

Foreshadowing as a device sketching the tragic doom of Romeo and Juliet can be found in the chorus (prologue) to the first act:

> From forth the fatal loins of these two foes
> A pair of star-cross'd lovers take their life; (Prol. 5–6)

Such foreshadowing is found in Romeo's lines as he makes his way to the Capulet ball:

> my mind misgives
> Some consequence yet hanging in the stars
> Shall bitterly begin his fearful date
> With this night's revels . . . (1.4.106–109)

Foreshadowing even finds its way into the joyous balcony scene when Juliet reflects:

> I have no joy of this contract to-night,
> It is too rash, too unadvis'd, too sudden,
> Too like the lightning, which doth cease to be
> Ere one can say it lightens. (2.2.117–120)

Imagery and Symbols

Because Shakespeare compresses the time of his main source, Arthur Brooke's *The Tragical Historye of Romeus and Juliet*, from nine months to five days (Sunday through Thursday/early Friday), there is plenty of time imagery. (Even Juliet's age is compressed from sixteen years to not quite fourteen.)

In the famous balcony scene, Juliet sees her love for Romeo as "too like the lightning," something that is over and done with very quickly. In this same balcony scene, the lovers mention the night eighteen times, the moon and stars thirteen times.[8] As Caroline Spurgeon first pointed out, Romeo and Juliet think of each other in terms of light in a rather dark world.[9]

Gunpowder is mentioned by both Romeo and Friar Lawrence, the latter using it to suggest the danger to which Romeo and Juliet's passion will lead. Shakespeare elaborated his source Arthur Brooke's use of fire and light images.[10]

As pointed out earlier, there are frequent religious images in the play, especially in the sonnet spoken by Romeo and Juliet at their initial meeting (1.5.93–106). Such figures show the purity of love between Romeo and Juliet as well as the dimensions that their passion has assumed almost instantly so as to become a religion unto them.

Themes

As might be expected, the themes of *Romeo and Juliet* reflect Shakespeare's other dramatic efforts of the 1590s. Apart from *Titus Andronicus*, Shakespeare overlooked tragedy and concerned himself with a great deal of English history and a great deal of comedy in this decade. That *Romeo and Juliet* is a twin to Shakespearean comedy has been pointed out by nearly every writer who has ventured to write about the play. We might therefore expect its major theme to deal with love. And *Romeo and Juliet* does deal with love—all kinds of love. There is the kind of love that Romeo is caught up in when we first meet him. This is the love based on his reading of Petrarch, an affected kind of love that trades in headaches for the sake of headaches. It is not much fun. This is the love that someone whom we never meet, named Rosaline, inspires. When the real thing comes along, Romeo recognizes it for what it is and gladly moves on from Rosaline—who, like Juliet, is a Capulet and may be taken as a kind of foil for her.

Romeo and Juliet's love can be contrasted with the lust that crops up in the comedic part of the play, that is, the first half of the play. This kind of love appears right off in the early bantering of the Capulet servants, Sampson and Gregory. There is a good deal more of it in the speeches of Juliet's nurse and Romeo's bosom buddy, Mercutio.

There is also the conventional kind of love in which "love has nothing to do with it." This is found in Capulet's efforts to arrange his daughter's marriage. To his credit, at first, he opposes doing so, since he feels that, at a bit less than fourteen, she is too young for talk of marriage and advises her suitor, Paris, to come around in two years.

It is this conventional love that brings in its train all the disasters that attend the true love of Romeo and Juliet. A marriage on paper never stacks up when compared to the kind that comes naturally. When the issue is forced, as it is by Capulet, trouble always follows.

The true love of Romeo and Juliet transcends the hardships brought on by it. They die, but their love is immortal. The transcending power of love is, as we have seen, one of the key themes of Shakespearean comedy.

Besides the transcendent power of love, the other theme developed throughout the 1590s—that of civil disorder found throughout the history cycles—finds its way into *Romeo and Juliet*. It is found in the brawling between retainers of the two families that leads off the play. Whenever Capulets and Montagues meet in the play, civil disorder is either at the forefront or on the horizon.

Leonardo DiCaprio and Claire Danes star as Romeo and Juliet in Baz Luhrman's 1996 adaptation of Shakespeare's tragedy.

Julius Caesar: The Misnamed Tragedy?

One of the first issues, if not the first issue, to be dealt with in Shakespeare's *Julius Caesar* is why the playwright named the play as he did. Since Julius Caesar dies midway through the play, the action winds up being carried out by other characters—chiefly Brutus and Mark Antony. Brutus is around until the final scene and Mark Antony lives throughout the entire play.

But if *Julius Caesar* is wrongly titled, it is not so much because Caesar dies in the middle of the play, but because he is not the play's real protagonist. Brutus is. And Brutus is still around in the fifth act. Yet it is Caesar's fame and legacy that pervade the play, together with his surrogate, Mark Antony, who defeats Brutus and Cassius at the Battle of Philippi.

Brutus anticipates Hamlet in that he is given to brooding and that he finds himself thrust into a difficult situation against his will. He is an idealist in a world that does not play by the rules. As far as understanding human nature, his enemy, Mark Antony, can run circles around him. As far as knowing how to survive, his friend and ally and coconspirator, Cassius, can shame him. But Brutus, like his great ancestor who rid Rome of a tyrant, is brave and commands our unqualified respect.

The Date of . . . ?

Since Francis Meres in his *Palladis Tamia* does not mention *Julius Caesar* in his list of twelve plays by Shakespeare written

Julius Caesar was a dictator who played a crucial role in the rise of the Roman Empire.

before September 1598, it may be assumed that this play was written no earlier than 1599. As it happens, there is some evidence for this date. A Swiss traveler in London in his notes dated September 21, 1599, describes a play about Caesar at a playhouse "over the water" (the Globe?), which can only be *Julius Caesar*.

Another allusion by the poet John Weever in a work published in 1601, but written as he says two years before, mentions the oration by Mark Antony in act 3, scene 2. We can be pretty certain, then, that *Julius Caesar* was on the boards by the late summer of 1599. While no doubt a popular play in Shakespeare's day, *Julius Caesar* was not published until the Folio of 1623—one of eighteen such plays that had to wait for the Folio before attaining publication. While this text appears to be based on a playhouse transcript, not all of the inconsistencies have been ironed out. It may even have been revised by Shakespeare.[1]

Like the other Roman plays, Shakespeare uses Plutarch as his source for *Julius Caesar*.

He Should Have Played Brutus

John Ford, the great film director, made a film in 1939 about Abraham Lincoln called *Young Mr. Lincoln*. Ford thought about having a scene in which Lincoln meets John Wilkes Booth but ultimately gave it up as being too much of a reach. Though Lincoln never actually met Booth, he did see him act. The play was *Julius Caesar* and Booth was supported by his two older brothers, Edwin and Junius Brutus. John Wilkes played Mark Antony. Lincoln, a big fan of Shakespeare and Byron, is said to have been impressed with the performances of the three Booths, the top in their field. Less than six months later, Lincoln would be assassinated by John Wilkes Booth.

Themes

Julius Caesar comes right where we might expect it, even if we could not be sure that it was written around 1599. It is part history and part tragedy. It is a twin of sorts to the English histories that have gone before and it is a near-kinsman to the great tragedies that will follow shortly after. As with most of the nine plays he had written previously on English history, *Julius Caesar* vividly depicts the chaos that follows when the head of state is slain. As with the tragedies to come, we see in Brutus someone whose temperament is ill-suited to the demands made upon it by the new circumstances that have arisen since the play's opening scene. Brutus might have lived to ripe old age if he had not conspired against Caesar. Doing so, he set in motion those forces which eventually destroy him at Philippi.

As usual, Shakespeare compresses actual time to squeeze all of the action into the two hours or so of a stage play. Caesar, for all his faults, was still Caesar, and he could only be replaced with another Caesar, as Brutus ironically is proclaimed by one of the mob (3.2.51). A strong ruling hand is necessary to rule the Rome of 44 BC. Factions will result only in civil war.

The mob is extremely fickle. Following Caesar's death, Brutus and Cassius are the heroes of the hour. After Antony's oration and his reading of Caesar's will, Brutus and Cassius are perceived as opportunists solely interested in their own welfare and not that of the Roman people. This plasticity of the mob mentality is something Shakespeare portrays again and again in his English history and Roman plays.

Style

Julius Caesar is one of Shakespeare's most poetic plays. It has an extremely high percentage of blank verse and only a small amount of prose.[2] There are no clowns in this play as there are in the comedies written at this same time. If there were, we might reasonably expect a song or two.

But instead of lyrics, Shakespeare imports something else into *Julius Caesar* that he learned from writing such a play as *As You Like It*. He learned the value of prose-set speeches from Rosalind and Touchstone in that play.[3] Shakespeare counterpoints such prose pieces against verse in the Capitol speeches of Brutus (3.2). Following Caesar's assassination, Brutus addresses the crowd in prose (3.2.12–47). This is directly contrasted by Antony's lyrical oration over Caesar's corpse. But it also is in opposition to the verse Brutus speaks just before and after it, suggesting that it is more contrived than felt. Prose is sparse in this play and when the leading character indulges in it, we have to wonder what it might mean.

> If there be any in this assembly, any dear friend of Caesar's, to him I say, that Brutus' love to Caesar was no less than his. If then that friend demand why Brutus rose

> against Caesar, this is my answer: Not that I lov'd Caesar less, but that I lov'd Rome more. Had you rather Caesar were living, and die all slaves, than that Caesar were dead, to live all freemen? As Caesar lov'd me, I weep for him; as he was fortunate, I rejoice at it; as he was valiant, I honor him; but, as he was ambitious, I slew him. (3.2.17–27)

Though full of memorable turns of speech, this oration does not reflect well on Brutus. It even ironically spells Brutus's deserved doom from Brutus's own lips. He is predicting his own downfall later in this famous speech. "I have done no more to Caesar than you shall do to Brutus" (3.2.36–37).

Metaphors abound in Brutus's language as well as in the one he talks to most—Cassius. Before the battle at Philippi, Brutus sees opportunity as a voyage on the sea:

> There is a tide in the affairs of men
> Which, taken at the flood, leads on to fortune;
> Omitted, all the voyage of their life
> Is bound in shallows and in miseries.
> On such a full sea are we now afloat,
> And we must take the current when it serves
> Or lose our ventures. (4.3.215–221)

Cassius's most striking figure in the play describes Caesar:

> Why, man, he doth bestride the narrow world
> Like a Colossus and we petty men
> Walk under his huge legs, and do peep about
> To find ourselves dishonorable graves. (1.2.134–137)

Characters

Brutus

Brutus is not a typical assassin. He takes plenty of convincing in order to "kill the foremost man of all this world." Cassius could kill Caesar easily enough, but he could not put a noble face on it. It is this nobility needed to grace Caesar's murder in the eyes of the masses that prompts Cassius to enlist Brutus in the plot to kill Caesar. Brutus is a thinking man—which makes him likable, if not overly accessible—but he is not streetwise. Idealist that he is and an aristocrat, he has no common ground that he shares with the masses.

Brutus, being a thinking man, is too sensitive to be a conspirator. He sums up his own self-destruction to be as well as the state's:

> Between the acting of a dreadful thing
> And the first motion, all the interim is
> Like a phantasma or a hideous dream.
> The Genius and the moral instruments
> Are then in council; and the state of a man,
> Like to a little kingdom, suffers then
> The nature of an insurrection. (2.1.63–69)

Through this speech, we are alerted to the trouble to come, when finally Caesar is assassinated. The speech embodies the major theme of the play in that it compares the strife going on in Brutus as he contemplates ridding Rome of Caesar to the chaos that will result upon Caesar's death.

Cassius

Cassius is Brutus's foil, his opposite. He is a man of action, not a thinker. He can take care of himself, but he cannot express anything loftier than envy until he shines in the tent scene:

Have you not love enough to bear with me
When that rash humor which my mother gave me
Makes me forgetful? (4.3.117–120)

Cassius is a good soldier. He wants to wait out Mark Antony and Octavius at Philippi. Brutus opposes this idea and Cassius submits to him. Cassius is right, as it happens. Antony and the ailing Octavius (in history, not the play) would have

Brutus stabs Caesar in a 1985 French production of *Julius Caesar*.

had to retreat in the case of a stalemate.[4] This only adds to our sense of fatal miscues from the conspirators' point of view, which began when Brutus allowed Mark Antony to speak in the Forum after Caesar's death. Cassius can manipulate Brutus's noble nature to get him to join the conspiracy, but afterward Brutus calls the shots. This, too, is ironically foreshadowed, when in a metaphor, Cassius says:

> You bear too stubborn and too strange a hand
> Over your friend that loves you. (1.2.35–36)

Cassius compares Brutus's recent treatment of him to a man reining in his mount.

Caesar

At the start of the play, it is evident from the way Shakespeare compresses time that Julius Caesar is perceived at least by some to be getting out of hand. He has made war, not only on foreign territories but on his fellow Romans as well. In short, Caesar runs a very real danger of becoming a tyrant—something that Rome has not seen for hundreds of years and something she never wants to see again. This is the point behind the discussion with Casca by Brutus and Cassius in act 1, scene 2, which conveys Antony's offer of a crown to Caesar repeated three times, and, while rejected, Caesar's heart does not appear to be behind the rejection. Again, Caesar's fast approach to tyranny is seen in the Roman Senate's decision to make him king everywhere but in Rome. And in the play's second scene, further evidence of Caesar's iron hand is seen in the fact that the two tribunes who had dispersed a crowd of his admirers and pulled down decorations from his statues all over Rome have been "put to silence."

Caesar's egotism and desire for the trappings of power are wonderfully revealed in his rejection of Metellus Cimber's

Ben Jonson's Gripe

Ben Jonson loved Shakespeare, as he said, "this side idolatry." But feisty Ben could be as critical of his friend as he was everyone else. He singled out a line, apparently from *Julius Caesar*, which he found ridiculous. The line in question went, "Caesar did not wrong but with just cause." The problem? The line does not actually appear in *Julius Caesar*. It may be that Jonson misremembered the line many years later when he mentioned his caveat or it may be that Shakespeare adjusted the line. At 3.1.47–48, Caesar tells Metellus Cimber, "Know Caesar doth not wrong, not without cause/Will he be satisfied." This is close to Jonson's line, but we'll never know if there was any revision.

appeal to have his brother returned from banishment. Caesar says:

> I could be well mov'd, if I were as you;
> If I could pray to move, prayers would move me;
> But I am constant as the Northern Star,
> Of whose true fix'd and resting quality
> There is no fellow in the firmament.
> The skies are painted with unnumber'd sparks,
> They are all fire, and everyone doth shine;
> But there's but one in all doth hold his place. (3.1.58–65)

But Caesar is not a one-dimensional monster such as the old morality plays painted. He is a keen judge of character, sizing up Cassius accurately in the "lean and hungry look" speech to Antony (1.2.193–209). He inspires love from Calpurnia and undying devotion from Antony (see the latter's soliloquy: 3.1.254–275).

Antony

Mark Antony certainly has a way with words—his speech in the Forum is the most celebrated one in the play (3.2.73–105):

> Friends, Romans, countrymen, lend me your ears.
> I come to bury Caesar, not to praise him.
> The evil that men do lives after them,
> The good is oft interred with their bones.
> So let it be with Caesar. The noble Brutus
> Hath told you that Caesar was ambitious.
> If it were so, it were a grievous fault,
> And grievously hath Caesar answered it. (3.2.74–81)

Antony's other gifts are not so alluring. He is cold, calculating, cruel, and deceptive. He will talk out of both sides of his mouth if it means getting his way and increasing his status, as he does with the conspirators in the first scene of act 3.

At the Capitol, Antony deals with Brutus rather than Cassius because he knows those traits that Brutus prides himself on and he plays these up. "Brutus is noble, wise, valiant and honest [honorable]" (3.1.126). Cassius is too shrewd a judge of character for Antony to try to butter up. Antony will check off the life of a nephew without batting an eye to please his fellow triumvirs (leaders of the Roman Republic) and then when one of them rises from the table to leave the room, begin instantly to arrange his loss of status. He will set the teeth of the Roman Republic on edge rather than give up his power. But in doing all these things, he is also advancing the deification of Caesar and showing duty to his friend's memory. It is left to Antony, also, to commemorate Brutus at the end of the play as "the noblest Roman of them all" (5.5.68).

Portia

Portia is Brutus's wife and appears in scenes 1 and 4 of the second act. She was the daughter of Cato the elder, who committed suicide following an unsuccessful struggle against Caesar's forces in 46 BC. Portia's death is mentioned in act 4, scene 3. Like her father, she is a suicide, having swallowed hot coals rather than see her husband killed by the Triumvirate. Her purpose in the play is to make Brutus more attractive to us in her concern for his welfare.[5]

Conclusion

Early in the seventeenth century, Shakespeare's happy comedies give way to a much darker mood in the playwright. This is reflected in *Julius Caesar*, where we see what Shakespeare could do with tragedy. Brutus is not quite Hamlet, but he is still a moody and reflective idealist. Brutus, like Hamlet, is loved and respected by everyone in the play, with the possible exception of Mark Antony. Even Caesar, up to the moment of his death, loves Brutus. His shock at finding Brutus numbered among the conspirators is seen when he says, "Et tu, Brute?"

Julius Caesar was written and performed in 1599 and it is thought that *Hamlet* followed soon after. In any case, *Julius Caesar* was on Shakespeare's mind when he wrote *Hamlet*.

9 Shakespeare's Incomparable *Hamlet*

Hamlet is Shakespeare's longest play. Uncut, it runs to more than four hours. Despite its length and despite the fact that Hamlet is center stage almost all the time, every actor aspires to play Hamlet. It stands as the pinnacle of the actor's career who undertakes to play it. *Hamlet* is also Shakespeare's most intriguing play. Questions abound. Why does Hamlet delay in his revenge against Claudius? Was he mad? Did he love Ophelia? Certainly, he could flirt with her and speak to her brother in hyperboles about his love after her death, but does he really love her? And when did Shakespeare write this play? The First Quarto (Q1) came out in 1603, giving us a very odd form of the play. But a play by this name was onstage as early as 1589.

Hamlet has been filmed so often in recent years that it should be familiar to almost everyone. Probably more everyday expressions come from this play than from any other work of literature. Almost every word of *Hamlet* is memorable, and we quote him and lesser characters in the play readily, often without knowing we are doing so.

We do not hesitate to speak of "something [being] rotten in the state of Denmark" (1.4.90), even though we may be standing in the state of New Jersey at the time. Often things are so quiet that "not a mouse is stirring" (1.1.11). If

Laurence Olivier plays the lead role in the 1948 film version of *Hamlet.* The actor also directed the Academy Award-winning film.

something is not working smoothly, we speak of there being "a rub" (3.1.65).

We not only quote Hamlet, but we quote Polonius and Gertrude as well. We quote Polonius when we offer that familiar saying of stage, screen, and television, "To thine own self be true" (1.3.78). We quote Hamlet's mother, Gertrude, the queen, when we talk of "sweets to the sweet" (5.1.241).

We know *Hamlet* to a degree that is remarkable for a play written more than four hundred years ago. It is as if the play has somehow entered our blood.

Date of *Hamlet*

Hamlet was written, most likely, in 1600–1601. Late in July 1602, the play was registered for publication and was published in a corrupt quarto in 1603. A much better quarto version of *Hamlet* was published in 1604–1605 (some surviving copies are dated 1604, others 1605). The First Folio (1623) would provide another good version of the play. Editors today depend on the latter two versions of the play as the basis for today's editions of *Hamlet*.

The quarto of 1603, usually referred to as the "Bad Quarto," sheds light on how Hamlet must have looked in performance. To take one example: In act 4, scene 5, as it stands today, there is a brief exchange between Hamlet's friend Horatio and Hamlet's mother, Queen Gertrude. Horatio has only one speech of two lines. One wonders what he is even doing there in the first place. Actually, he is urging the queen to speak with the distraught Ophelia. At this point in the play, there is hardly anyone else who could do this task. Hamlet, Rosencrantz, and Guildenstern are on their way to England; Laertes is in France and Polonius is dead. But in the Bad Quarto, the exchange between the queen and Horatio takes place much later in the scene and is expanded. It is much more appropriate and therefore suggests that this was how it was played on the stage originally.[1]

Style

The Elizabethan stage did not go in for scenery much. Without scenery to move around and, provided actors knew the eight hundred or so lines they committed to memory each day, plays could be done in the two hours that custom has allotted them.[2] An example of how figurative language could save on scenery and backdrops is found when Horatio speaks in act 1:

> But look, the morn in russet mantle clad
> Walks o'er the dew of yon high eastward hill. (1.1.171–172)

A motion picture studio today would have to spend thousands on stock footage by traveling second unit crews to accomplish what Horatio here does in two lines of dialogue—to announce that morning has broken.

Hamlet, for the most part, makes use of blank verse that is end-stopped. There are five iambic feet in most lines. Sometimes, however, the blank verse line is varied, usually by switching the accented syllable in the first or second foot from the second syllable to the first. A good example of this, evincing personification in the process, is found in the third scene of act 1:

> ˘ / / ˘ ˘ / ˘ / ˘ /
> The wind sits in the shoulder of your sail (1.3.56)

It is in the second foot of this line that the normal blank verse meter is reversed with the accented foot preceding the unstressed one SITS in.

When Shakespeare uses rhyming couplets, it is usually to put the audience on notice that a scene is about to end.

Sometimes, as with Friar Laurence in *Romeo and Juliet* (2.3.1–26), it is done to spice up what might otherwise be a dull monologue. But in *Hamlet*, Hamlet chides his mother with this pointed reply:

> A bloody deed—almost as bad, good Mother,
> As kill a king, and marry with his brother. (3.4.27–28)

This neat rejoinder on Hamlet's part sums up what has been on his mind throughout the play. Shakespeare, by using this rhyming couplet amid unrhymed blank verse, is bidding the queen (and us) to pay special attention to Hamlet's words.

Still, a fair amount of prose is introduced in this play, notably when Hamlet talks with the touring players (2.2, 3.2). He speaks to his schoolfellows, Rosencrantz and Guildenstern, in prose, and when he is not quoting some old ballad, he speaks prose to Polonius. The reason for the prose passages on Hamlet's part is two-fold. 1) Hamlet uses prose to assume his "antic disposition," making for some humorous exchanges with Polonius, the upshot of which will find its way back to Claudius. 2) Prose is a means of relaxing for the prince. With Claudius, Hamlet speaks in verse, as though always on cue, having a necessity always to be sharp as a tack. To get away from this, he finds prose a sort of release and indulges it as often as possible.[3] Hamlet, who is at odds with virtually everyone around him, engages in repartee a great deal and this, too, is in prose. There is an extended bout of repartee between Hamlet and the first gravedigger (5.1) and then the other.

Hamlet thinks aloud in verse, however. Such sessions of internal debate are found in his seven famous soliloquies. These allow the audience to know the innermost workings of Hamlet's mind. When Hamlet speaks prose to Ophelia or

Polonius, for instance, he may well be pulling her or his leg, but in his soliloquies, he is thoroughly honest with his feelings. We can take his word in these. It is as though in these soliloquies, he is confiding to his diary. No one who keeps a diary sets down a lie in it. Hamlet's soliloquies are the best tool we possess in our understanding of his character.

Shakespeare did not take long in his development to make use of the soliloquy. Already in so early a comedy as *The Two Gentlemen of Verona*, Proteus pauses in his deceitfulness long enough to soliloquize, for example (1.1.63–69). Gloucester (later, Richard III) has a number of soliloquies in the three plays in which he is a leading character. The soliloquies can easily be identified by their first lines, e.g., "O, what a rogue and peasant slave am I!"(2.2.550–607) and "'Tis now the very witching time of night" (3.2.390–407).

The most famous of all Hamlet's soliloquies is, of course, found in act 3, scene 1 (lines 56–87). It begins:

> To be, or not to be, that is the question:
> Whether 'tis nobler in the mind to suffer
> The slings and arrows of outrageous fortune,
> Or to take arms against a sea of troubles,
> And by opposing, end them. To die, to sleep—
> No more, and by a sleep to say we end
> The heart-ache and the thousand natural shocks
> That flesh is heir to; 'tis a consummation
> Devoutly to be wish'd.

Symbols and Imagery

Numerous types of images can be found in *Hamlet*. There is the imagery of disease and pestilence. There are images of poison or venom, appropriate in a tragedy in which five characters die of poisoning. War imagery is prevalent in the

THE "TO BE OR NOT TO BE" SOLILOQUY Q1

The First Quarto (Q1) of *Hamlet*, published in 1603 and called the "Bad Quarto," gives a decidedly different version of the play than the one we are accustomed to. Among the most radical differences between the first published version of the play and later versions concerns the "To Be or Not To Be" soliloquy, probably the most famous speech in Shakespeare. Here is how the speech appears in the First Quarto:

> To be or not to be, ay there's the point,
> To die, to sleep, is that all? Ay all:
> No, to sleep, to dream, ay marry there it goes,
> For in that dream of death, when we awake,
> And borne before an everlasting judge,
> From whence no passenger ever returned,
> The undiscovered country, at whose sight
> The happy smile, and the accursed damned.
> But for this, the joyful hope of this,
> Who'd bear the scorns and flattery of the world,
> Scorned by the right rich, the rich cursed of the poor?
> The widow being oppressed, the orphan wronged,
> The taste of hunger, or a tyrant's reign,
> And thousand more calamities besides,
> To grunt and sweat under this weary life,
> When that he may his full quietus make,
> With a bare bodkin, who would this endure,
> But for a hope of something after death?
> Which pulses the brain, and confounds the sense,
> Which makes us rather bear those evils we have,
> Than fly to others that we know not of.
> Ay that, O this conscience makes cowards of us all.[4]

play and the acting profession is alluded to time and time again. Fortune accounts for a number of images and, along with it, harlotry, which ties in well with the play's concern with appearance versus reality. (In the playlet, with its high-flown language, Fortune is referred to as a strumpet.) Fortune's wheel is alluded to by Rosencrantz suggesting that Majesty is a wheel which, when it falls, takes down the state (3.3.15–23).

Hamlet, in keeping with the appearance-versus-reality theme of the play, is preoccupied with appearances from his first two or three speeches on. Gertrude's grief is, in his view, too easily followed by her marriage to Claudius. His shabby

In this illustration, Hamlet speaks to the king's ghost in act 1, scene 4. Behind Hamlet are Marcellus and Horatio.

treatment of Ophelia in the play is really his resentful treatment of his mother extended to the girl, whose innocence Hamlet feels to be an act.

In the unfolding of its plot, *Hamlet* makes use of poison at every turn (as also with *Antony and Cleopatra*). Hamlet's uncle Claudius has poisoned the elder Hamlet before the play starts. In the preceding show and as part of the action of the playlet, *The Murder of Gonzago*, there is more poisoning. Gertrude dies by poison, Laertes dies by poison, the king dies by having poisoned wine forced down his throat, following a stab wound, also full of poison. Finally, Hamlet dies by the poisoned tip of Laertes's rapier.

The disease imagery bespeaks the sickness of the realm due to the usurpation of majesty. This is a common theme throughout Shakespeare's career and in *Hamlet*, it recurs because of the murder of Hamlet's father by his uncle. Hamlet's insanity, real or feigned, also contributes to the disease imagery in the play.

War images are appropriate in a play that is essentially a warfare between Claudius and Hamlet. Curiously, when Hamlet refers to the ghost as "a worthy pioneer" (1.5.171), he alludes to a miner, especially someone who digs tunnels during the siege of a town or fortress. Small wonder that many readers of Shakespeare credit him with military service abroad.[5] It must not be overlooked that Fortinbras accords Hamlet a soldier's funeral rites.

As for imagery from the acting profession, this results from the great significance of the Mousetrap playlet, which is the pivotal scene of *Hamlet*. In it the king undeniably reveals his guilt.

Themes

Appearance versus reality, a favorite theme of Shakespeare's, is a major theme of *Hamlet*. We encounter it in one of Hamlet's first speeches when he says to his mother:

> Seems, madam? nay, it is, I know not "seems."
> 'Tis not alone my inky cloak, good mother,
> Nor customary suits of solemn black,
> Nor windy suspiration of forc'd breath,
> No, nor the fruitful river in the eye,
> Nor the dejected havior of the visage,
> Together with all forms, moods, shapes of grief,
> That can denote me truly. These indeed seem,
> For they are actions that a man might play,
> But I have that within which passes show,
> These but the trappings and the suits of woe. (1.2.76–86)

Another major theme in *Hamlet*—a favorite Shakespearean theme, found throughout his career—is the evil that comes upon a state when the ruler is corrupt. In *Hamlet*, however, the evil in Hamlet's own nature has to surface in order to deal with the evil in Claudius and the evil brought on the state by him. The evil in Hamlet surfaces in his dealings with Ophelia under the guise of his "antic disposition" and is even more forcefully demonstrated when he kills Polonius (3.4).

Death is a prevalent theme in *Hamlet*. Death is evident from the first scene involving a ghost, to the last act with the gravedigger tossing bones about, to the deaths finally of most the major characters in the play. Hamlet muses upon the progress of a dead body, even a great one like Alexander's or Caesar's, ultimately becoming a mere stopper in a hole (5.1.207–217). His recurring thoughts about suicide and Claudius's needful damnation also reflect his preoccupation with death.

Latin and Ghosts

"Thou art a scholar; speak to it."

In the opening scene of *Hamlet,* Marcellus, a sentinel, urges Horatio to deal with the ghost in these words. There is a very good reason for this. Unlettered persons, so it was believed, were likely to say the wrong thing to a ghost and thus anger it. A scholarly type such as Horatio supposedly knew the tactful approach to speaking with a ghost. Furthermore, he knows Latin. Latin was believed to be the last resort when encountering ghosts. If the spirit was revealed to be an evil one, Latin was the language used to exorcise it.[7]

Hamlet and Freud

Around the turn of the twentieth century, the intellectual world was abuzz with talk of suppressed desires and the Oedipus complex. By 1911, Freud and Oedipus had been applied in masterly fashion to Hamlet.[6] Does Hamlet suffer from an Oedipus complex? According to this theory, Hamlet resents his father (and by extension, Claudius) because of his own suppressed desire for his mother. After his father's death, Hamlet is cool and distant to his uncle, even before the ghost has revealed the cause of his death. Hamlet sees that his uncle has taken his father's place with his mother. His delay in exacting vengeance on Claudius could thus be explained as his realization that his uncle is merely doing what he has unconsciously desired to do himself.

In late 1922, John Barrymore's tremendously successful *Hamlet* opened on Broadway. The "closet scene" between Hamlet and Gertrude (3.4) seemed to some critics to imply very strongly that Hamlet was under the influence of an Oedipal complex. This view gains some credence when one considers that the actress who played Gertrude, Blanche Yurka, was actually five years younger than Barrymore and thus more suitable to portray his lover than his mother.[8]

Characters

Hamlet

Hamlet is quite possibly the most fully realized portrait of a human being in literature. We enter into his thoughts by means of soliloquies a number of times in the play. He has our attention and that of everyone onstage at all times. His striking language and startling wit are remarkable and perhaps unprecedented in drama. His sense of purpose and sense of direction are extraordinary. He can shun Ophelia, whom he has loved in the past, and he can "speak daggers" to his mother in order to get to the bottom of Claudius's guilt.

His doubts about his uncle's character are only intuition at first. Later, after seeing the ghost and witnessing the key play-within-a-play, and especially after seeing Claudius at prayer, Hamlet knows that he must get his revenge on the king. That he hesitates and does not kill Claudius when he has the chance is one of the most scrutinized and dissected moments in all of drama. "Now might I do it pat," he says (3.3.73), but he also wants to send his victim to Hell. To kill Claudius at his prayers is not the way to send him from this world in Hamlet's view. Because he does not do so, seven other people will die, including Hamlet himself.

Claudius

Claudius is the archrival of young Hamlet. He has killed Hamlet's father, married Hamlet's mother, and rules Denmark

WHAT'S WITH THOSE PIRATES?

Hamlet as swashbuckler? In a scene (4.6) omitted in the First Quarto of *Hamlet,* but found in the Second Quarto and the Folio, Hamlet's friend reads a letter from him. The letter tells of Hamlet's boat, headed to England, being intercepted by pirates. Not only this, but when the two ships grappled, he boarded the pirate vessel alone. The pirate ship then returned Hamlet to Denmark. The letter has occasioned "much throwing about of brains," among scholars the last century and a half. Was Hamlet's boarding of the pirate ship just plain headstrong or did he somehow collude with the pirates? Speaking of the pirates, Hamlet tells Horatio, "But they knew what they did. I am to do a good turn for them" (4.6.20–21). Was the "good turn" in return for taking Hamlet back to Denmark? As you read this play, see what you think about Hamlet's capture by the pirates.

in her place and his. Hamlet, therefore, has a threefold reason to disapprove of Claudius and from the very beginning he does. What their relations were like when old Hamlet was up and around we can only guess. Probably uncle and nephew did not see eye to eye about much, unless it would be some flattery directed at Hamlet senior by his brother. Claudius would have always stood in the elder Hamlet's shadow.

But Claudius is an able ruler. He handles the Fortinbras crisis skillfully and diplomatically. He is also able to think on his feet, as when Laertes leads a revolt on the palace (4.5). He not only thwarts this action, he makes an ally of his would-be assailant.

Laertes, I must commune with your grief,
Or you deny me right. Go but apart,

Make choice of whom your wisest friends you will,
And they shall hear and judge 'twixt you and me,
If by direct or collateral hand
They find us touched, we will our kingdom give,
Our crown, out life, and all that we call ours,
To you in satisfaction. But if not,
Be you content to lend your patience to us
And we shall jointly labor with your soul
To give it due content. (4.5.199–209)

This 1852 painting by John Everett Millais depicts Ophelia's drowning as described in act 4, scene 7 of *Hamlet*.

Ophelia

Ophelia is the very soul of suffering. In love with Hamlet, she loses her father to his vagaries and, after her death, her brother. Whatever interest Hamlet showed her before the play begins is basically gone before her first appearance onstage. Ophelia is at her best in her one scene with her brother before he goes off to Paris to study (1.3).

She is an innocent who drowns wearing a wreath of flowers while climbing a tree over a weeping brook. Her madness springs from the brutal death of her father by the man she loves. Her brother at the time is away, and she has no one to turn to for support. Under the weight of her grief, she willingly sinks in the stream.

Gertrude

It is Gertrude's hasty marriage to Claudius so soon after his father's death that plants the seed of Hamlet's rage at the beginning of the play. Hamlet's worst fears about his mother are confirmed by the ghost (1.5.42–52). It is Gertrude's unfaithfulness to his father that makes Hamlet forswear his faith, not only in her, but Ophelia as well. As there are no other major female characters in the play, Hamlet's disdain for these two amounts to misogyny. In the closet scene of act 3, scene 4, Hamlet upbraids Gertrude for her love for Claudius. As the ghost appears to Hamlet in this scene, but is not seen by her, this suggests her unworthiness as a mate.

Horatio

Horatio is Hamlet's sole confidant. Hamlet is alienated from everyone around him with the exception of Horatio and the actors who tour Denmark. After Hamlet's death, it is Horatio who must set the record straight concerning the prince's life

"YOURS PERHAPS TOO CANDIDLY"

Actor John Barrymore took his highly successful Broadway *Hamlet* to London in 1925. The great British dramatist George Bernard Shaw attended a performance and afterward wrote Barrymore a letter about it. Shaw had his gripes about Shakespeare, preferring Shakespeare's problem plays to *Hamlet*, but he did not like anyone messing with Shakespeare. Shaw claimed to have known the characters in Shakespeare's plays before he knew the kids in his neighborhood.

When Barrymore made cuts in *Hamlet* and inserted additions of his own, Shaw was outraged and said so in a letter he signed, "yours perhaps too candidly, G. Bernard Shaw."

and death. Horatio is objective and dispassionate, which Hamlet admires in him (3.2.56–75). This also makes him something of a butt of ridicule, however, when the ghost appears to the watch and he is shaken.

Polonius

Polonius likes to meddle in other people's business. He sets Reynaldo to spy on his son Laertes while he is away at school. He uses Ophelia to spy on Hamlet, something he does himself with the king when he can. His murder in the closet scene is the death warrant for Hamlet. No longer can the young prince appear to be confused and innocent. He has chosen the path of a cold-blooded murder and, as such, is irredeemable.

Polonius, though meddling and foolish, has lines that are among the most quoted of the play. His advice to Laertes is a case in point:

> This above all, to thine own self be true,
> And it must follow, as the night the day,
> Thou canst not then be false to any man. (1.3.78–80)

Polonius is essentially a comic character and his interplay with Hamlet is engaging in act 2, scene 2, which leads to his famous appraisal of Hamlet's antic behavior:

> Though this be madness, yet there is method in't. (2.2.205–206)

Because Polonius is so often foolish and foppish, his brutal death—like Mercutio's in *Romeo and Juliet*—alerts us to the fact that the threshold that separates comedy from tragedy has been reached.

Laertes

Laertes is like Hamlet in a number of ways. He is therefore a foil to Hamlet. He, too, loses his father to murder, something he must avenge. He is a student in a foreign land, and he is the object of his father's spies, even as Hamlet is spied on by both old school chums and Polonius. Unlike Hamlet, Laertes is quick to take action against those he distrusts. He subdues the palace in his anger at Claudius for what he takes as his part in the death of his father. Laertes's skill with the rapier overshadows Hamlet's in that he is given a handicap in the fencing match (5.2.280–310), but his skill is more apparent than real as Hamlet quickly scores two points on him. This is another example of appearance versus reality with which the play and Hamlet are concerned.

Fortinbras

Fortinbras means "strong-in-arm" in French. George Bernard Shaw said that he never once saw a production of *Hamlet* in which Fortinbras appeared.[9] Shaw should not have complained. No one sees much of Fortinbras in any production. In act 4, scene 4, he has just two speeches, although at the very end of the play he has twice that number of speeches, including the last of the play. That's all anyone sees of him. Yet his presence is felt from the very first scene on. Fortinbras is Hamlet's foil—like Laertes. Like Hamlet, Fortinbras has lost his father before the play commences. Like Hamlet, he seeks to avenge his dead father. Fortinbras perhaps detects a side of Hamlet that most people overlook when, at the end of the play, he orders that Hamlet be given full military rites at his funeral.

Conclusion

Hamlet, of course, is a dark tragedy. In order to face the evil of his uncle, Hamlet is corrupted by evil himself. He has to embrace evil in order to force the goblet's contents down the king's throat. Worse yet, he kills a silly old courtier for little more than eavesdropping.

Hamlet is the most famous play ever written. So much of our everyday speech comes from this play. It has been the most esteemed of Shakespeare's tragedies ever since it was first published in a rough form in 1603. But, lately, scholars have questioned whether it is Shakespeare's greatest tragedy. They have looked beyond *Hamlet* to the other tragedies, and in *King Lear* they think they may have found Shakespeare's most perfect work.

10 Shakespeare's Other Tragedies

Shakespeare's plays usually have a source that we can point to at a distance of more than four centuries. His tragedies are no exception. But did his tragedies have an extra dimension to them other than a printed source?

One of the favorite scholarly pursuits at the turn of the last century was trying to discover the reason Shakespeare turned out one great tragedy after another in quick succession three centuries earlier.[1] After *Julius Caesar* in 1599, there would be no more comedies, certainly no more "happy comedies." *Hamlet* was written around 1600–1601. *Othello* was acted by 1604 and therefore written perhaps a year or two earlier. *Macbeth* was written around 1605 and *King Lear* probably a year later. Scholars have wondered whether something profoundly disturbing happened to Shakespeare at the turn of the sixteenth century.

To be sure, things happened around that time. The popular Earl of Essex, a close friend of the Earl of Southampton and possibly known to Shakespeare, led an uprising against the queen, which ended disastrously in February 1601. The earl was executed and Southampton was imprisoned for the rest of Elizabeth's reign (something that may be glanced at in Sonnet 107).[2] When the queen died two years after the rebellion, no lamentations from Shakespeare's pen followed. He remained silent and was later rebuked for it.[3]

More personally, Shakespeare's father died in September 1601. This in turn was only five years after the death of his son, Hamnet, and the two deaths may have led to a change in the poet's outlook. Hamnet, it must be said, was Shakespeare's only male heir and the son he hoped would continue his line and name.

No doubt all of this had an effect on Shakespeare's writing—particularly the tragedies.

Othello

Othello is interesting to modern audiences and readers because of its concerns with race. Othello is obviously a black man, which Roderigo's description at the outset of the play makes clear (1.1.65). He is a man full of honor, valiant but innocent and unsophisticated enough to be preyed upon and manipulated by the incredibly sinister Iago. Othello is reminiscent of Brutus in that he is easily manipulated.

Othello's strongest images derive from the sea. It is the sea he values next to Desdemona:

> But that I love the gentle Desdemona,
> I would not my unhoused free condition
> Put into circumscription and confine
> For the sea's worth. (1.2.24–27)

In the following passage, the rhythm of the verse imitates the billowing of the ocean waves:

> If after every tempest come such calms,
> May the winds blow till they have waken'd death!
> And let the laboring bark climb hills of sea
> Olympus-high and duck again as low
> As hell's from heaven! (2.1.183–187)

Paul Robeson's *Othello*

African-American actor Paul Robeson had his first crack at performing *Othello* in London in 1930, when he was thirty-two. He had garnered good reviews and had worked with two actresses who would go on to become dames of the United Kingdom—Sybil Thorndike and Peggy Ashcroft. Robeson had yet to take his *Othello* to America, however. When he did in 1942–1943, the world was steeped in World War II and segregation was the norm throughout the United States. For an African-American actor to work with a white actress, as man and wife, was unheard of. Clearly, *Othello* presented a production company with major headaches. It was decided to put the play on off-Broadway at first, to test the waters. This was done in college towns like Cambridge, Massachusetts, the home of Harvard University. The result can best be seen in critic Elliot Norton's review:

> I remember when the innocent, vulnerable Desdemona prepared for bed, that magnificent scene, the tension was enormous, and when he strangled her, it was pretty close to unbearable. At the end, there was a moment of absolute silence, unlike almost anything I've ever seen or heard in the theatre. And then absolute pandemonium by that first audience in Cambridge, overwhelming acceptance, an historic occasion. . . . They had done something wonderful and everyone knew it and everyone rejoiced.[4]

Robeson's *Othello,* with Jose Ferrer as Iago and Uta Hagen as Desdemona, enjoyed a long run on Broadway—in fact, it set a record of 296 performances.

Later, Othello, in a frenzy, again reverts to imagery from the sea:

> Like to the Pontic Sea,
> Whose icy current and compulsive course
> Nev'r keeps retiring ebb, but keeps due on
> To the Propontic and the Hellespont,
> Even so my bloody thoughts, with violent pace,
> Shall nev'r look back, nev'r ebb to humble love,
> Till that a capable and wide revenge
> Swallow them up. (3.3.456–463)

Othello's vow to Iago in the climactic action of the tragedy shows how inflexible Othello can be when his mind is made up. He is as unyielding as the sea. Unfortunately, such inflexibility leads to the tragic resolution of the play in Desdemona's suffocation by her husband (5.2). Interestingly, Shakespeare interrupts Desdemona's murder by a knocking on the door, the same device he will later use in *Macbeth* with the knocking on the gate when Duncan is killed by the Macbeths.

Othello's most famous line comes at the end of the play when he knows he has been duped by the heinous Iago. This man of action stands unarmed before the world, his soul bared:

> Speak of me as I am. Nothing extenuate,
> Nor set down aught in malice. Then must you speak
> Of one that loved not wisely but too well;
> Of one not easily jealous, but, being wrought,
> Perplexed in the extreme; of one whose hand,
> Like the base Judean, threw a pearl away
> Richer than all his tribe . . . (5.2. 342–348)

Paul Robeson plays the lead role in the 1943–1944 stage production of *Othello*. In the final scene of the play, Othello kills his wife after mistakenly believing she has been unfaithful.

King Lear

King Lear was first published in 1608. It was probably written sometime after 1605, the year the eclipses mentioned in the play by Gloucester (1.2.103–104) took place. It is based on Holinshed, as all of Shakespeare's British plays are, as well as an old anonymous play, *The Tragedie of King Leir and his Three Daughters*. This play, unlike Shakespeare's, ends happily.

The theme of *King Lear* is redemption through suffering. Only in his banishment from his two unloving daughters does Lear realize how much suffering humanity undergoes. He says:

> Poor naked wretches, wheresoe'er you are,
> That bide the pelting of this pitiless storm
> How shall your houseless heads and unfed sides,
> Your looped and windowed raggedness, defend you
> From seasons such as these? Oh, I have ta'en
> Too little care of this! Take physic, pomp.
> Expose yourself to feel what wretches feel,
> That thou mayst shake the superflux to them
> And show the heavens more just. (3.4.28–36)

Gloucester has a bitterer epiphany when he says:

> As flies to wanton boys are we to the gods,
> They kill us for their sport. (4.1.37–38)

As with *Hamlet*, there is plenty of disease imagery in *Lear*. Insanity, ebbing and flowing in Lear's case or feigned in Edgar's, is vividly depicted in the play. The Fool assists us in understanding this in his sometimes cryptic, sometimes scathing, comments on Lear's foolishness. The disease imagery ties in with Cornwall going off to die after being wounded by a servant and Regan's being poisoned by her sister. Afterward, the brain-sick Goneril commits suicide.

Sex-charged imagery is also found throughout *King Lear*. Edgar, as Tom O'Bedlam, tells of his illicit affair with his master's wife as the source of his troubles (3.4.84–99). The villainous Edmund is the result of an unlawful union of Gloucester and his mistress. Even legitimate procreation is blasted by Lear:

> Crack nature's molds, all germens [seeds] spill at once
> That make ingrateful man! (3.2.8–9)

Throughout the play the very disorder of Nature is seen. The servant who kills Cornwall is a symbol of Nature being turned upside down. In the natural scheme of things, servants did not rebel against their masters. The fact that Lear's daughters have turned him out is the height of disorder. In addition to the unnaturalness of being cold and inhuman to the man who has given them life, they have also been disloyal to their king. The upheaval of Nature mentioned by Titania due to her quarrel with Oberon in *A Midsummer Night's Dream* (2.1.87–117) is but a light pleasantry compared to the disorder found in *King Lear*.

Structure of *King Lear*

King Lear in many ways resembles a comedy, at least so far as its structure is concerned. It utilizes a commentator in the Fool, as does *As You Like It* with Jaques and Touchstone. It goes from the court to the wilderness back to the court as does *A Midsummer Night's Dream* and *As You Like It*. It makes use of disguise as seen in Edgar's donning the habit of the roguish beggar, Tom O'Bedlam.

Macbeth

Macbeth was written sometime between 1603 and 1606. Some allusions, if not late afterthoughts, suggest a date between

November 1605 and the summer of 1606 at the earliest. The play is based on two stories from *Holinshed's Chronicles* (1587 ed.). Though not published until the Folio of 1623, the play was certainly on the stage by April 20, 1611, when the astrologer Simon Forman wrote a description of it in his diary. At twenty-five hundred lines, it is the shortest of Shakespeare's tragedies.

Macbeth is a study in evil. The evil is studied on two fronts—the personal evil of Macbeth and his wife and the political evil arising from an unjust and illegitimate ruler. The play tells the story of a Scottish noble (thane), who begins the play as wonderfully brave and loyal to his king in putting

This 2015 production of *King Lear* was staged in Toronto, Canada.

down an insurrection and invasion. Macbeth is awarded the title of a thane executed for treason. Ironically, Macbeth will act out the same ambitions of the traitor whose boots he fills.

Macbeth's impulse toward evil arising from his own ambition is assisted by the prophesies of the three Weird Sisters. He meets with these women a number of times during the play and each time he is encouraged in his descent into evil by their prophesies. In the end, Macbeth will realize the futility of his trust in such creatures and be reduced to a life that is meaningless and without support of any kind.

Macbeth is thus the story of a total moral collapse. In fact, this play is the only one of Shakespeare's great tragedies in which the protagonist is a villain. He is reminiscent, therefore, of that other great historical villain (in Shakespeare's view) Richard III, a story Shakespeare chronicled more than a decade before he turned to Macbeth. Like *Richard III*, *Macbeth* is a play of prophesies and ghosts. The protagonists of both plays die lonely and bloody deaths. Indeed, images of blood pervade *Macbeth*. The other predominant imagery of the play, as we might expect of one of this kind, deals with darkness (deeds that will not bear light), Nature in turmoil, and water (suggesting the ceaseless efforts by Macbeth and his lady to wash themselves clean of their guilt). In one revealing passage (1.5.17–19), Lady Macbeth tells her husband that he lacks "the illness" that should attend ambition. She means that he is not wicked enough to follow through on his desires.

Though evil is triumphant in the battle for Macbeth's soul, it comes only after a struggle that is evident throughout the play. Macbeth and Lady Macbeth do not give up their humanity easily. Instead, they lose it piece by piece. At the same time, Lady Macbeth will do just about anything to aid her husband. She will unsex herself in an effort to be more brutal

(1.5.40–42). She would dash out her own baby's brains on her husband's behalf (1.7.54–59). Ultimately, neither Macbeth nor Lady Macbeth ever derive an ounce of satisfaction from their moral compromise.

Macbeth is one of Shakespeare's most quotable plays and was a favorite of Abraham Lincoln.[6] One of the play's most notable speeches is Macbeth's realization of how empty all his evil ambition has been:

> Tomorrow, and tomorrow, and tomorrow
> Creeps in his petty pace from day to day,
> To the last syllable of recorded time,
> And all our yesterdays have lighted fools
> The way to dusty death. Out, out brief candle!
> Life's but a walking shadow, a poor player
> That struts and frets his hour upon the stage
> And then is heard no more. It is a tale
> Told by an idiot, full of sound and fury,
> Signifying nothing. (5.5.19–28)

The occasion of this speech is Macbeth's learning of the suicide of his wife, Lady Macbeth. His isolation has proceeded apace throughout the play—he kills his friend Banquo, an ally MacDuff deserts him—and now, with the death of his wife, it is all brought home to him.

In this speech, Shakespeare compares life to an actor, but not a very good one. Perhaps he has in mind one of those ranting fellows that had to have permission of his father to play the guild hall in Stratford when he was growing up. Along with acting, we see a metaphor based on the other half of Shakespeare's professional persona—storytelling. Again, like the actor, the writer or bard is not very good. His tale is the composition of an idiot and has no meaning. Macbeth, at this point, has no one to turn to. He realizes that the Weird Sisters have played him false with twisted prophesies regarding his future greatness. All that is left for him is to die fighting.

Titus Andronicus

Following the great tragedies were two Roman plays, *Antony and Cleopatra* and *Coriolanus*. These were based on Plutarch, as was the earlier *Julius Caesar*. Shakespeare began writing tragedy with a play set in Rome but not based on Plutarch's *Lives*. This earlier play, not usually classified as a Roman play due to its fictional origin, was *Titus Andronicus*. It was the first of Shakespeare's plays to be published—in early 1594, in an edition that was lost to scholars until December 1904.

Titus is a grim play. It is what scholars call a "tragedy of blood"—a type of drama popular when Shakespeare began his career. Each horror depicted onstage is succeeded by a worse one. In *Titus Andronicus*, fully fifteen deaths occur, onstage and off.[7] This record was enough to ensure that the play would be produced regularly in a day given to a love of violence.

Titus Andronicus lost its appeal a generation or two after Shakespeare's day. It was spurned by scholars for many years as unworthy of Shakespeare.[8] However, since it was included in the First Folio and mentioned by Francis Meres as Shakespeare's in 1598, it is hard to see how it could not be by Shakespeare. In 1999, *Titus Andronicus* was made as a film by Julie Taymor. It starred Sir Anthony Hopkins and Jessica Lange and was simply called *Titus*.

Antony and Cleopatra

Antony and Cleopatra was supposed to be published in 1608, but if an edition came out then, no copy has survived. The entry in the Stationers' Register does at least establish that the play had been written by May 1608, the time of the entry. This great tragedy first saw print in the First Folio, seven years after Shakespeare's death.

Along with *Romeo and Juliet*, *Antony and Cleopatra* is Shakespeare's great tragedy of love. It differs from the earlier tragedy in being more character driven and in the nature of the love. Antony and Cleopatra are much too suspicious of each other to be Romeo and Juliet. In fact, Cleopatra seems about to desert him when Antony commits suicide. But Antony's suicide is not a clean one. He falls on his sword but continues to live and cannot get anyone to finish the job. He then learns that Cleopatra is yet alive and has sent for him. He goes to her, or rather, is carried to her and lives long enough to speak seven speeches with this queen of Egypt.

> I am dying, Egypt, dying, only
> I here importune death awhile until
> Of many thousand kisses the poor last
> I lay upon thy lips. (4.15.19–22)

Antony dies during a speech by Cleopatra. He also dies before the last act.

Antony and Cleopatra continues the story begun in *Julius Caesar*. Now, Octavius and Antony are at odds, due to Antony's dalliance with the queen of Egypt. A hasty marriage to Octavius's sister by Antony does little to clear up the distrust. Lepidus still figures as the third member of the Triumvirate, but he has little importance in this second play.

Besides *Antony and Cleopatra*'s ups and downs, this play has other scenes that are notable. The son of Pompey the Great, for example, who is the common enemy to the Triumvirate, is advised by his henchman that he could kill the triumvirs while they are on his ship discussing a truce. Pompey declines, citing his honor in a backhanded way:

> Ah, this thou shouldst have done,
> And not have spoke on't! In me 'tis villainy,
> In thee 't had been good service. Thou must know
> 'Tis not my profit that does lead mine honor,
> Mine honor, it. Repent that e'er thy tongue
> Hath so betrayed thine act. Being done unknown,
> I should have found it afterward well done,
> But must condemn it now. (2.7.73–80)

This speech and the incident behind it are at the root of the action. In order to get ahead in the Roman world of *Antony and Cleopatra*, throats had to be cut, whether that of Antony's nephew in *Julius Caesar* or that of a fellow triumvir, Lepidus, or an enemy fled to Egypt, Sextus Pompey (Pompey). That Pompey missed his chance to climb over the dead bodies of his enemies can only be considered foolish in the context of the play.

This tragedy utilizes, of all things, a clown. He brings the asps to Cleopatra in the final scene so that she may commit suicide. He speaks prose, after the manner of all Shakespearean clowns, and a lot of it. It is almost too much for Cleopatra to bear in her time of trouble. It is almost too much for readers and spectators to bear, too, since it totally breaks the tragic spell. The clown says silly things like "his biting is immortal: those that do die of it do seldom or never recover" (5.2.245–247). After a number of such speeches, the clown takes his leave and Cleopatra prepares to die.

That the clown appears in the play when he does—right at the point of Cleopatra's death—lessens the sting of the asps when finally Cleopatra applies them. It gives the tragedy a moment of levity at a time when it is consummating a marriage, that of the dead Antony and the soon-to-die

Katherine Hepburn performs the lead female role in a 1960 production of *Antony and Cleopatra*.

Cleopatra. This is appropriate, too, since comedy traditionally ends in a marriage.

Cleopatra says:

> Husband, I come.
> Now to that name my courage prove my title! (5.2.285–286)

In *Antony and Cleopatra*, Shakespeare seems to have experimented with a tragedy that is not wholly tragic. Like the comedies, *Antony and Cleopatra* shows us the transcendent power of love as it overcomes the powers marshaled against it. Antony loses the world for Cleopatra and she does the same for him, but in the end they have each other. In that, they (and love) have triumphed.

Timon of Athens

Timon of Athens was first published in the Folio of 1623. In places, it seems more like a rough draft than a finished play, for example the page and Fool (2.2) and the conflicting epitaphs (5.4), and does not fit in with Shakespeare's other plays. It has been classed as both a comedy and a tragedy and shares elements with both. There are no certain allusions to outside events, making the play hard to date. About the only means of establishing a date lies in the fact that its source, like *Antony and Cleopatra*, lies in Plutarch's discussion of Antony and Alcibiades. It is therefore usually dated 1606–1608.[9]

Timon of Athens is a morality play in which characters represent types. Timon represents generosity at first, then extreme emptiness at the end. No one in the play is anything more than a symbol. The steward represents faithfulness. Fair-weather friends, such as the poet and the painter, represent hypocrisy. Alcibiades, while an outcast like Timon, is a foil to him since he learns the power of mercy and its use in an evil world. Though Timon dies, the play ends on a note of hope and reconciliation due to the growth of Alcibiades's character.

Timon of Athens has more prose than other plays so late in Shakespeare's career.[10] When Timon rails, it is usually in verse, but one exception occurs when Timon is bantering with the play's resident cynic, Apemantus:

> If thou wert the lion, the fox would beguile thee; if thou wert the lamb, the fox would eat thee; if thou wert the fox, the lion would suspect thee, when peradventure thou wert accused by the ass. If thou wert the ass, thy dulness would torment thee; and still thou livest but as a breakfast to the wolf, If thou wert the wolf, thy greediness would afflict thee, and oft thou shouldst hazard thy life for thy dinner, Wert thou the unicorn, pride and wrath would confound thee, and make thine own self the conquest of thy fury, Wert thou a bear, thou wouldst be killed by the horse; wert thou a horse, thou wouldst be seized by the leopard; wert thou a leopard, thou wert germane to the lion, and the spots of thy kindred were jurors on thy life, All thy safety were remotion [removal], and thy defense absence. What beast couldst thou be, that were not subject to a beast and what a beast art thou already, that seest not thy loss in transformation! (4.3.330–347)

This speech is cyclic, ending where it begins. Though prose, its logical construction can be set up thus to resemble verse. It relates that Apemantus is a beast to begin with before all the transformations imposed on him by Timon.

Coriolanus

Coriolanus is the third and last of Shakespeare's so-called Roman plays. It was written around 1608 and was first published in the Folio.[11]

With *Coriolanus*, Shakespeare again resorted to Plutarch for material for the stuff of great tragedy. He fashioned a hero whom we can admire for many of his qualities but who, after all, loses his good sense when provoked. In this play, Shakespeare looks at the perversion of love as seen early on between Coriolanus and Cominius, another general. Coriolanus says:

> O! let em clip ye
> In arms as sound as when I wooed; in heart
> As merry as when our nuptial day was done,
> And tapers burned to bedward. (1.6.29–32)

Aufidius, the sworn enemy of Coriolanus, welcomes him into his camp upon his defection from Rome in much the same language:

> Know thou first,
> I loved the maid I married; never man
> Sighed truer breath; but that I see here,
> Thou noble thing, more dances my rapt heart
> Than when I first my wedded mistress saw
> Bestride my threshold. (4.5.116–121)

From these passages, it is evident that in this play the god of war carries more weight than the goddess of love and, worse yet, the two are often confused. Even Coriolanus's mother shares in this perverse love for valor:

> I tell thee, daughter, I sprang not more in joy at first
> hearing he was a man-child than now in first seeing he
> had proved himself a man. (1.3.15–18).

Coriolanus lends itself to widely varying political interpretations. To some, Coriolanus's sneering at the commons repeatedly suggests autocracy. Democracy is not to be trusted, at least in time of war. Others have seen the play as putting down fascism.[12]

Conclusion

The great tragedies follow in the wake of *Hamlet* and the problem plays. *Othello*, *King Lear*, and *Macbeth* depict tragic heroes. Othello, like Brutus before him, is a good man easily led astray by someone with selfish motives. Macbeth and Lady Macbeth have the beginnings of a conscience, but only enough to make life miserable for them while they keep compounding their crimes. Lear lacks judgment, but he makes up for it in his growth following his banishment to the heath.

These tragic protagonists are full-figured parts for the actors playing them. Much as we might like a character such as Romeo, there is more tragic depth in Brutus or Coriolanus for the actor. Actor Richard Burton, for example, made a fine Hamlet but never had any interest in playing Romeo.[13] This is not to say that *Romeo and Juliet* is not a great play, but only that in these later plays Shakespeare's tragic vision has become more character-based than before. These later heroes owe their doom to something within which they cannot control. It is their nature that underlies their tragedy.

There would be no more tragedies after *Coriolanus*. Shakespeare was ready to try something new. He was ready to blend tragedy with comedy, resulting in the so-called "tragicomedies," categorized by later scholars as the romances.

11

Not Exactly This or That: The Romances

Following the comedies and tragedies, Shakespeare took up a new type of drama that was a mix of comedy and tragedy. This drama we now call romance, but such a term was not used in Shakespeare's day. It may be that this new drama was forced onto Shakespeare by the popularity of a writing duo, Francis Beaumont and John Fletcher. However that was, Shakespeare certainly left his unmistakable stamp on it.

By 1608, Shakespeare's acting company, now called the King's Men, had a winter theater—the Blackfriar's playhouse. It was an indoor playhouse, lit by torches and chandeliers and thus suited for performances at night, which in the winter came on early. The audience at this playhouse was of a different sort than those who resorted to the outdoor playhouses. The Blackfriar's audience was wealthier, more sophisticated, and more educated than the patrons of the Globe and other public playhouses.[1] In fact, apprentices were a large part of the audiences of the public playhouses and they were, in fact, incurring the wrath of the Lord Mayor and the aldermen by attending the theater when they were supposed to be at work.

Shakespeare was forty-four in 1608 and near the end of his playwriting career. The happy comedies and the farces were behind him. He had only recently finished up with the tragedies. Next would be the romances. Part tragedy, part comedy, there are five of them: *Pericles*, *Cymbeline*, *The Winter's Tale*, *The Tempest*, and *The Two Noble Kinsmen*.

Shakespeare is depicted here with a group of his contemporaries, many of whom were also writers.

The romances, together with the late history, *Henry VIII*, share a number of common themes, such as redemption through suffering and reconciliation after separation. *The Winter's Tale* and *The Tempest* involve the supernatural in a big way, though all the romances are colored by it—even the late history, *Henry VIII*. One romance, *Pericles*, deals in part with incest, a sign that the days of the happy comedies were indeed over.

The period covered by the composition of the romances ranges from 1608–1613. Most, if not all, were written for the Blackfriars indoor theatre. Of the five plays, only *Pericles* was published in Shakespeare's lifetime and it was published in a most unsatisfactory quarto. *Pericles* is the only romance—indeed, the only play—by Shakespeare that derives solely from a bad text. *Pericles* twice saw publication in 1609 as quartos and twice more in 1611 and 1619. But it was omitted from both the First Folio and Second Folio.

Heroines

Young heroines are the center of attention in the romances, with the exception of *The Two Noble Kinsmen*, which concentrates on the friendship of two young men. In *Cymbeline*, Imogen rates as one of Shakespeare's most delightful heroines, cut from the same cloth as Portia in *Merchant* and Rosalind in *As You Like It*. In *The Winter's Tale*, Perdita is shamelessly young and incredibly wise for her sixteen years. In *Pericles*, Marina is the tempest-tossed heroine, not glimpsed until late in the play. Miranda is the heroine of *The Tempest* and, but for Juliet, the youngest of Shakespeare's heroines. Though exposed to the reptile-like witch's son, Caliban, all through her youth, she has a high opinion of mortals nevertheless.

The Renewal of Life Theme

The importance of youth to these heroines ties in well with one of Shakespeare's unifying themes in his romances—renewal of life after a great crisis. This, of course, is precisely the point of the comedies, too. Marina in *Pericles* and Perdita in *The Winter's Tale* do not so much as appear in their plays until the fourth act, long after the major action of the play has gotten under way. It is their job to prepare for a hopeful future of reconciliation and redemption at the conclusion of these plays.

In *The Winter's Tale*, this perception is facilitated by the use of a chorus at the beginning of the fourth act, which speaking in the person of Time, makes it clear that the tumult of the first three acts will be dispelled in the last two. Perdita's betrothal to Florizel in the first scene of act 5 brings together the two men who have been at odds throughout the play.

Pericles

Pericles is the first of the romances. Among the oddities of its publishing history is the fact that it did not show up as Shakespeare's work until its appearance in the Third Folio (second issue) in 1664. Here, it was joined by six other plays deemed by scholars to be apocryphal (that is, doubtfully Shakespeare's).

Pericles sets the tone for the romances to follow. The hero is beset with tremendous adversity and separated from those he loves most for long periods of time, believing these loved ones to be dead. Then, at the climax of the play, the loved ones return, as if arisen from the dead, and a new life for the principal characters begins. (In *The Winter's Tale*, one character does not survive to take part in the final reunion and renewal, but even here the pattern is the same.) Pericles, alone of all the heroes to issue from the romances, suffers his losses and misfortunes passively without having brought them on his own head through rashness, jealousy, or pride.

Cymbeline

Cymbeline was probably the next of the romances. There is no text prior to that of the First Folio. A performance of the play, probably at the Globe, was taken in by the astrologer Simon Forman in 1611. *Cymbeline*, therefore, is usually dated about 1609–1610.[2]

Shakespeare read about Cymbeline, as he read about all other British history, in *Holinshed's Chronicles* (1587, 2nd ed.). Only there, however, the king is known by his Roman name, Cunobelinus.

Cymbeline, like Caesar in the play named for him, is not the center of attention in his own play. He is a peripheral figure, though hardly marginal. His daughter, Imogen, and her two long-lost brothers are the play's true focus. The main plot revolves around the romance between Imogen and Posthumus—a young man not worthy of his wife.

At the heart of *Cymbeline* is the wager (1.5). In exile in Italy, Posthumus is overbearing in his pride of Imogen's virtue and foolishly allows himself to bet on it. Iachimo ("little Iago" in Italian; "little Jack" or "Jackie" in English) challenges his boast and goes to Britain to spy on Imogen. He hides in a trunk in her bedroom. He thus can inventory everything in her room and even on her person. He even snatches a bracelet from her wrist for good measure.

Iachimo convinces Posthumus that Imogen has been untrue to him and the latter sets about to have her killed. In a story that involves a potion and assuming a disguise, Imogen is finally reunited, not only with her brothers but with her exiled husband as well.

As described above, Iachimo places himself in a trunk in Imogen's bedroom. He thinks aloud as he surveys the room, noting somewhat surprisingly that the crickets outside are chirping. In keeping with this stealth and silence, Iachimo makes use of sleep-inducing sibilants in his monologue:

> The crickets sing, and man's o'erlabored sense
> Repairs itself by rest. Our Tarquin thus/ Did softly
> press the rushes, ere he wakeken'd/ The chastity that he
> wounded. (2.2.11–14)

The *s* sounds are frequent in this line and a half and establish at once that it is late at night and very quiet in the vicinity. Numerous contractions in the speech as a whole (2.2.11–51) establish that Iachimo is in a hurry. The bracelet seems to be giving him trouble as he slips it off so that he barely seems to keep a civil tongue in his head, no matter the volume (2.2.33–34).[3]

The Winter's Tale

The Winter's Tale was seen by astrologer Simon Forman in May 1611 at the Globe. It is likely very late in Shakespeare's career, probably third or fourth from the last of his plays. It is a tragicomedy, involving the death of little Mamillius, the son of Leontes and Hermione, as well as the death, by a ravening bear, of the courtier Antigonus. Death, indeed, is always on the horizon from the opening scene on. The source of the play's conflict is the unreasonable jealousy of Leontes, king of Sicilia.

Among the memorable characters in *The Winter's Tale* is a rogue named Autolycus. He is one of those rogues that Shakespeare seems to have especially enjoyed creating. The most lyrical of Shakespeare's rogues, Autolycus charms us even as he scares the shepherd half to death with accounts of torture.

But musical as Autolycus can be, the best song in the play is Perdita's:

. . . daffodils,
That come before the swallow dares and take
The winds of March with beauty; violets, dim,
But sweeter than the lids of Juno's eyes
Or Cytherea's breath; pale primroses,
That die unmarried ere they can behold

The Intriguing Blank Verse of *Cymbeline*

In *Cymbeline,* Shakespeare broke with the past and gave his blank verse a new look. He would give this new pattern a tryout in this play and employ it to even better effect in his next, *The Winter's Tale.*[4]

Imagery in these jerky lines is not Shakespeare's aim here. It is instead the actual shape of the line itself. Notice he carefully avoids the end-stopped line in favor of shorter phrasing, often pausing twice within a line of verse. Lines look like free verse more than blank verse and they sound like stream of consciousness. Imogen's soliloquy at the beginning of act 3, scene 6 illustrates Shakespeare's new line pattern:

O Jove, I think
Foundations fly the wretched—such, I mean,
Where they should be relieved. Two beggars told me
I could not miss my way. Will poor folks lie,
That have afflictions on them, knowing 'tis
A punishment or trial? Yes. No wonder,
When rich ones scarce tell true. To lapse in fullness
Is sorer than to lie for need, and falsehood
Is worse in kings than beggars. (3.6.6–14)

Bright Phoebus in his strength—a malady
Most incident to maids; bold oxlips and
The crown imperial; lillies of all kinds,
The flow'r-de-luce being one: Oh, these I lack,
To make you garlands of, and my sweet friend,
To strew him o'er and o'er! (4.4.118–129)

The Tempest

The Tempest was played at court in November 1611. It is based on a number of accounts describing the shipwreck experienced by the ship *The Sea Venture* off the coast of Bermuda in 1609. Two accounts of this colonizing expedition (intended to breathe fresh life into the tottering Virginia colony) appeared the next year. From these sources, Shakespeare conceived the idea that the New World was a sort of Paradise. It was not inhabited by devils as rumor had it. Since all the participants of the colonizing expedition survived, Shakespeare found the New World benevolent. And so it appears in *The Tempest*.

Shakespeare is concerned with quite a number of things in *The Tempest*. Indeed, to a large number of critics and commentators, its complexity marks the pinnacle of Shakespeare's dramatic career. Every emotion available to human beings is on display in this play and at the end there is a satisfying catharsis (dramatic relief) as the sometime magician, sometime ruler of Milan, Prospero, relinquishes his magic and returns to rule his duchy. The play begins with a shipwreck, remarkable, as Mark Twain noted, for its "sailor talk."[5]

As with the other romances, Shakespeare is concerned in *The Tempest* with reconciliation and rejuvenation. The divine workings of Providence underlie all the action of the play and its happy outcome.

This illustration of the opening shipwreck scene of *The Tempest* was included in Nicholas Rowe's 1709 publication of Shakespeare's plays.

In Caliban (and the two buffoons who join his conspiracy) there is plenty of humor. But Caliban symbolizes something more than crass humor. He is representative of mankind in its natural state. Whatever the New World meant to Shakespeare, natural man needed work. The civilizing influence of culture, especially Christian culture, was necessary to offset the primitive appetite of natural man. (Caliban had once tried to rape Miranda and his name is an anagram for "cannibal.")

The Tempest ends warmly, preceded by Prospero's famous epitome:

> Our revels now are ended. These our actors,
> As I foretold you were spirits and
> Are melted into air, into thin air;
> And, like the baseless fabric of this vision,
> The cloud-capped towers, the gorgeous palaces,
> The solemn temples, the great globe itself,
> Yea, all which it inherit, shall dissolve,
> And, like this insubstantial pageant faded,
> Leave not a rack behind. We are such stuff
> As dreams are made on, and our little life
> Is rounded with a sleep. (4.1.148–158)

The play utilizes the pageantry of the masque, a theatrical form popular in the early seventeenth century. This art form is thoroughly appropriate for a play which is steeped in magic. At one point, for example, the king of Naples, who has been seeking his son, Ferdinand, suddenly sees Ferdinand and Miranda appear before him (5.1). This ties in well with a favorite theme of Shakespeare's—appearance versus reality.

Probably no play by Shakespeare deserves to be staged more than *The Tempest*. Like all the romances and the late history, *Henry VIII*, much of the action is found in the stage directions. In the case of *The Tempest*, it is a good thing that this is so, since it is apparently meant to be a short play. It is Shakespeare's second shortest, in fact.

The Tempest has a fair percentage of prose and one thing must be noted about it. In the wonderful storm scene that opens the play, everyone is speaking prose, usually cursing his luck or the man next to him. Then, most of the characters begin to speak verse. One man, however, does not. He is old Gonzalo, one of the good characters in the play. The fact that he continues to speak prose while the others are speaking fragments of verse distinguishes him from the others.

At another point (2.1), the characters onstage are speaking prose. The king of Naples enters and they begin to speak in blank verse, even Gonzalo. This is done out of respect for his kingly person—it is customary for characters to use their most exalted language in his presence.

The Two Noble Kinsmen

The Two Noble Kinsmen dates from 1613, after February, since a masque that appears in the play was acted at court in that month.[6] This was at a time, therefore, when Shakespeare had returned to Stratford to live. It is probable, then, that his part in the composition of *The Two Noble Kinsmen* was not a large one. Still, there are similarities between this play and a much earlier one—*A Midsummer Night's Dream*. Both plays employ the device of the wedding of Theseus and Hippolyta to begin the action. In *Kinsmen*, the jailer's daughter frees Palamon from his imprisonment, feeds him, and hides him away in the woods in an effort to gain his love (2.5). This is reminiscent of what Helena does at the end of the opening scene in *A Midsummer Night's Dream* in hopes of regaining Demetrius's love. There is also a hint of *Hamlet*'s Ophelia in the madness and songs of the jailer's daughter.

The Two Noble Kinsmen did not appear in print until 1634, eighteen years after Shakespeare's death. It appeared as a paperback quarto, with pages numbered in the modern way and even with acts and scenes designated. These last, though, are broken up at different points than modern editions of the play. The quarto was registered and published as being "by John Fletcher and William Shakespeare." Such external evidence makes it apparent that Shakespeare did not write the whole play. All one need do to be certain of this is to read the Epilogue.

The source of *The Two Noble Kinsmen* is "The Knight's Tale" in Chaucer's *Canterbury Tales*. The play deals with two cousins, Palamon and Arcite, who fall in love with Hippolyta's sister, Emilia. Their friendship is strained by this circumstance and they end up fighting a duel. Arcite wins the duel and as Palamon prepares to be executed, Arcite is mortally wounded after falling from his horse. The dying Arcite gives Palamon and Emilia his blessing.

As with the other romances, *The Two Noble Kinsmen* deals with nobility and honor. It involves the supernatural, as seen in act 5 when Emilia makes a sacrifice to Venus, which results in a rose tree dropping a single rose. It ends, as do the others, on a note of reconciliation and forgiveness.

Conclusion

The romances blend tragedy and comedy. Their endings have the improbability of comedy, yet there is the inevitability of a better future for those who have undergone such difficult journeys. They are survivors—Pericles and Marina, Prospero and Miranda, Leontes and Perdita and, especially, Imogen—and we take heart in the fact that they have overcome the odds against them. The same deck that is stacked against them is, after all, stacked against us. We realize when reading the romances that what the protagonists have to overcome in these plays is what we all are up against in our daily lives—the urge to give up because life is simply too hard. Yet they do go on and so do we all. It would be Shakespeare's final message to his audiences and readers.

Shakespeare: Then and Now

Shakespeare has been dead for four centuries. Since his death in 1616, Shakespeare's reputation has undergone some ups and downs. Certainly, Shakespeare was a name to be reckoned with in his day, and to prove it his fellow actors John Heminges and Henry Condell brought out the First Folio, containing thirty-six of his plays, seven years after his death. This sort of thing had only been done once before when Ben Jonson's works had been collected in 1616. But after the publication of Shakespeare's Second Folio in 1632, things started to take a dip, not only for Shakespeare but the English drama as a whole. The English Revolution was under way in the 1640s and the Puritans, very hostile to drama, were in power. The second Globe playhouse was pulled down in 1642, and thereafter, plays had to be performed on the sly.

Finally, in 1660, with Charles II seated on the British throne, the Restoration took place and drama was very much in again. But a new type of drama was at the forefront. This drama looked to the continent for inspiration and followed Aristotle's unities of time and place. Shakespeare was still performed but heavily adapted. Highly popular plays in the past, like *A Midsummer Night's Dream*, seemed silly to some veteran playgoers while less popular plays, like *Troilus and Cressida*, began a new life.

It was in the Restoration that actresses began to grace the English stage. In Shakespeare's day, the parts of girls and women were played by boys. In time, actresses would reverse the past altogether and play male roles. Great actresses, such as Sarah Bernhardt and Dame Judith Anderson, would assume that pinnacle of acting roles, Hamlet.

Publishing Shakespeare

Shakespeare's plays were published in 1709 by Nicholas Rowe, with a brief biography of the poet by actor Thomas Betterton. Rowe's edition proved so successful that, before long, others took Shakespeare's plays in hand. Alexander Pope published an edition in 1725, taking the liberty of placing what he thought was unworthy of Shakespeare at the bottom of the page. Not that Pope blamed Shakespeare for such vagaries—it was the actors who were guilty. Pope made enemies almost for a living, and it was shortly after his edition came out that the most prominent of Pope's enemies, Lewis Theobald, brought out a rival edition of Shakespeare.

For the rest of the eighteenth century and much of the nineteenth, rival editions and warring editors were the norm. Sometimes this rivalry led editors to fabricate material that they thought would make their edition stand out from the competition. This was done by George Steevens in a small way in the eighteenth century and by John Payne Collier in a big way in the nineteenth. In fact, it was not that long ago that leading American editions included a poem as possibly Shakespeare's, which the leading British edition would have nothing to do with. In turn, that edition had a poem of its own that the American editions shunned.[1] The present era of Shakespeare publication is definitely one of adventure wherein plays and poems, long secluded in the shadows, have been brought to

In 1899, Sarah Bernhardt starred in a controversial but popular stage adaptation of *Hamlet*.

the forefront as worthy at least of publication in a collected edition of Shakespeare.

The Two Noble Kinsmen, studied in this book, was first published in 1634 as by John Fletcher and William Shakespeare. No edition of Shakespeare carried the play for two centuries and then only as a "doubtful play." The play went into the editions of John Fletcher and Francis Beaumont, known as Beaumont and Fletcher, beginning with their Second Folio in 1679. But, finally, in 1936, with the Kittredge and in the 1960s, with the Signet Classic, *The Two Noble Kinsmen* was brought into the Shakespeare fold, where it has remained ever since. A similar fate, at present, seems to be involved with *King Edward III*.

In recent years—actually, about the past fifty years—computers have had a say in what is and what is not Shakespeare. For instance, in the mid-1990s, a poem, *A Lover's Complaint*, was dismissed by a team of computer-aided researchers from the canon of Shakespeare's works. More recently, again using computers to show how many times Shakespeare used or didn't use a certain word, leading scholars have made what seems an airtight case for Shakespeare's authorship of the poem.[2] But with this poem, something else is involved. The poem in question was originally put out by a publisher who had also printed a spurious poem, attributed to a certain "W.S." This same publisher had also published the *Sonnets*. There matters would remain as a sort of standoff if one didn't know that, along with the *Sonnets*, the publisher printed *A Lover's Complaint*. Common sense would seem to indicate that the publisher got both works from the same source—Shakespeare's own manuscript.

An interesting avenue that scholars have taken up recently concerns Shakespeare's intention when writing his plays. Of course, he wanted to entertain audiences with his "two-hours traffic of the stage." But was something else involved when he wrote? Early plays, like *Richard III*, middle ones, like *Hamlet*, and late plays, like *Cymbeline*, all take a good deal longer than can be played in the traditional two hours normally reckoned for a presentation in the Elizabethan or early modern age. Could it be that he wanted his plays to be read in the study as well as acted on the stage? Scholars are beginning to think so. Support for this view is found in the fact that sometimes publishers in Shakespeare's days put quotation marks (commonplace markers) around passages deemed important or worthy of putting down in a commonplace book.[3]

SHAKESPEARE IN THE COMPUTER AGE

In his *Groatsworth of Wit* (1592), Robert Greene refers to someone he calls "Shake-scene," who dabbled in playwriting and apparently helped himself to portions of other men's work when writing on his own plays. Scholars have wondered whether Shakespeare was Greene's "Shake-scene." Along with this, they have wondered if Greene really was the author of the *Groatsworth*. In 1970, Warren C. Austin, working with an IBM computer, found that the *Groatsworth*, as far as vocabulary, usage, and style go, fits the work of Greene's editor, Henry Chettle, much better than Greene himself. Even though Austin's case has won almost unanimous approval among scholars, the *Groatsworth* is still referred to as Greene's *Groatsworth*. As for "Shake-scene," William Shakespeare is by far the leading candidate as the victim of the attack. Here, again, is a mystery since Chettle and Shakespeare seem to have gotten along and may, indeed, have worked together in the old play *Sir Thomas More*.

Shakespeare on Film

By the beginning of the twentieth century, Shakespeare took on a whole new life, which even he might not have ever been able to imagine. Whereas before he was enjoyed either in the theater or on the page, now he took on a whole new life on film. Oddly enough, when it came time for Shakespeare's interaction with this powerful medium, it was not the hugely popular favorites like *Romeo and Juliet* or *Hamlet* that made it to celluloid first but, rather, the early history play, *King John.* Only a portion of the play, starring Sir Herbert Beerbohn Tree, was filmed in 1899. Probably the reason a history play was the first Shakespeare filmed has to do with the large casts customary in the histories as well as the amount of spectacle—coronations, court scenes, and battles. It was this aspect, by the way, that got the original Globe Theatre burned down in 1613. During a performance of the play, cannons, loaded with burning cotton wadding were shot off and caught the thatch roof of the playhouse on fire. Nobody was hurt, but one man whose pants caught on fire had the good fortune to be drinking from a half-gallon tankard of ale and used that to put the fire out.

Shakespeare could always use color and sound, and he got it in due time, but not before a beautiful black-and-white *Romeo and Juliet* was made in 1936, starring Leslie Howard and Norma Shearer and directed by George Cukor. And though color was becoming the norm in films by 1948, Laurence Olivier chose to make his award-winning *Hamlet* in black and white. In that same year, too, Orson Welles made a notable *Macbeth*, also in black and white.

Kenneth Branagh has led the way in filming Shakespeare. His range takes in *Henry V* (1989) to comedies, like *Much Ado*

About Nothing (1993) and *Love's Labour's Lost* (2000), to *Othello* (1995) and an uncut four-hour *Hamlet* (1996). Some of his films have traditional sets and costumes while *Hamle*t takes place in eighteenth-century Russia and *Love's Labour's Lost* is set in 1930's Hollywood as a musical!

canon

The body of work by an author.

Shakespearean films have not been confined to English-speaking nations. Russia produced a very outstanding *Hamlet* in 1964, which was adapted by novelist Boris Pasternak of *Doctor Zhivago* fame. The great Japanese director Akira Kurosawa made films of *Macbeth*, *Hamlet*, and *King Lear*. His *Macbeth* (*Throne of Blood*, 1957) and *Lear* (*Ran*, 1983*)* are probably best known.

But often, Shakespeare's stories are adapted, modernized, and introduced to a new audience. *O* (2001) (based on *Othello*) starring Julia Stiles and Mekhi Phifer, and *10 Things I Hate About You* (1999) (based on *The Taming of the Shrew*), starring Heath Ledger alongside Stiles were both adapted to take place in high school, with teenagers as their main characters. *She's the Man* (2006) starring Amanda Bynes and Channing Tatum is based off of Shakespere's *Twelfth Night*. Even Dinsey was not immune to adapting Shakespeare. The popular animated film *The Lion King* (1994) is based on Shakespeare's *Hamlet*.

Broadway Musicals have also found themselves borrowing from the bard. Cole Porter's musical *Kiss Me Kate* (1948) was a success based, once again, on *The Taming of the Shrew*. But perhaps the most successful musical adaptation of Shakepeare's work was Leonard Bernstein and Stephen Sondheim's *West Side Story* (Broadway debut in 1957, adpted into film in 1961). It brought *Romeo and Juliet* into the twentieth century, with the lovers on opposite sides of a gang dispute in New York City.

Once in a while, Shakespeare biography gets on film. This was the case in 1998 when *Shakespeare in Love* was made, starring Gwyneth Paltrow and Joseph Fiennes. The film was cowritten by Tom Stoppard, who had a very successful stage hit, *Rosencrantz and Guildenstern Are Dead*, thirty years before. *Shakespeare in Love* is a highly fictionalized biography with Joseph Fiennes as a very intense, energetic young Shakespeare. Probably the hardest thing about the film to believe is that Shakespeare, who wrote at least two plays a year, ever had a bout with writer's block. This movie is memorable because it may be the only time that quasi-mystical theater entrepreneur Philip Henslowe (portrayed by Geoffrey Rush) can be found on film.

Not that Shakespeare has had it all his own way. The Oxford theory (claiming Edward de Vere as the "real" Shakespeare) was broached by actor Leslie Howard, in *Pempernel Smith* (1941) a year before he died, and in 2011, *Anonymous*, a very elaborately produced film, was released, also espousing the Oxford cause.

Shakespeare Comes to America

In 2014, James Shapiro collected pieces by Americans on Shakespeare in an anthology called *Shakespeare in America*.[4] The pieces include four by American presidents, including a charming foreword by former President Bill Clinton. Ralph Waldo Emerson's famous essay on Shakespeare is found in the collection as well as a comic bit on the Authorship Controversy by Woody Allen.

America has had plenty to say about William Shakespeare. In fact, we have done our level best to get anything he left

Kenneth Branagh has brought many Shakespeare works to modern audiences. In 1993 he directed and starred in the film version of *Much Ado About Nothing*. The cast included (clockwise from top) Keanu Reeves, Denzel Washington, Branagh, Emma Thompson, Kate Beckinsale, Robert Sean Leonard, and Michael Keaton.

behind. On each coast can be found a library housing rare books by or about Shakespeare. In Washington, DC, there is the Folger Shakespeare Library. In San Marino, California, the Huntington Library is another such lodestone for Shakespeare scholars. The Folger has more Shakespeare folios that any other institution in the world. The Huntington houses one of only two known Q1's of *Hamlet.* Harvard, Yale, the Newberry Library in Chicago, the University of Illinois at Urbana, and the University of Texas have valuable and unique artifacts connected with Shakespeare.

Though Shakespeare was born and raised in Stratford-on-Avon and worked in London and was thoroughly English,

STAY TUNED

The search for anything connected with Shakespeare goes on. No manuscript survives, though 107 lines of a manuscript play, *Sir Thomas More,* are generally accepted as Shakespeare's. No letters from him survive, only a puzzling will in which no books or manuscripts are mentioned. Most of his estate went to his elder daughter, Susanna, and her husband, Dr. John Hall. Hall left a will in which he bequeathed his books and manuscripts to Thomas Nash, the husband of the Halls' only child, Elizabeth. Could any of Shakespeare's books and papers have been included in Hall's bequest to his son-in-law? In the late 1960s, Shakespeare biographer S. Schoenbaum wanted to find out. After scouring England and Scotland, he came up empty. Still, something of enormous value, concerning Shakespeare's life and work, is bound to turn up. There are plays and poems out there that we don't know who wrote. It may be that some of these will gain the consensus of scholarly opinion and be included among the poet's work in time.

The Folger Shakespeare Library in Washington, DC, houses the world's largest collection of Shakespeare works.

that has not stopped America from trying to get its hands on one of his pallbearers. Such was said to be the case for a man buried in a Fredericksburg, Virginia, cemetery. Unfortunately, this hoax was exposed by Sir George Greenwood in 1916.[5]

The Bard in the Twenty-First Century

With the Information Age here, the study of Shakespeare has taken on new dimensions. We can pull up old quartos and folios and see what plays looked like to readers of Shakespeare four centuries ago.[6] We can see the odd spellings and lack of punctuation typical of the era. We wonder whether such was the habit of Shakespeare or the printer or the age. Of course, more modern editions of Shakespeare, complete in a single volume or accessible through the Internet, are available to anyone with a PC or a library card. And theatergoers can easily refer to Twitter, Facebook, and other social media sites to find out what is being played and when and where.

This widespread availability of Shakespeare has influenced how his works are taught (and learned). High school students can podcast their own versions of Shakespeare, adapting such with contemporary music. You don't have to be a Broadway star these days to get your licks in with Shakespeare. A hands-on approach has always been the best way to learn anything, and that is the way with learning Shakespeare now more than ever.

And why, after four centuries, does the whole world embrace Shakespeare? Possibly it's because whatever we have thought and whatever we have felt and whatever we will ever think or ever feel, he said.

Chronology

1564– William Shakespeare is born (traditional date is April 23; baptized April 26).

1582– Marries Anne Hathaway on November 28.

1583– First child, Susanna, is born.

1585– Twins, Hamnet and Judith, are born; Shakespeare's "lost years" begin.

1593– *Venus and Adonis* is entered in the Stationer's Register; plague hits London and keeps playhouses closed most of this year and part of the next.

1594– Publication of *Titus Andronicus*, *The Rape of Lucrece*, and *2 Henry VI* under name of *The First Part of the Contention Betwixt the Two Famous Houses of York and Lancaster* (This was a bad quarto.); *The Comedy of Errors* is performed at Gray's Inn (a London law school).

1595– *3 Henry VI* is published in corrupt form as *The True Tragedy of Richard, Duke of York.*

1596– Shakespeare's only son, Hamnet, dies at age eleven.

1597– Publication of *Richard II*, *Richard III*, and bad quarto of *Romeo and Juliet*.

1598– *1 Henry IV* is published sometime after February 25; *Love's Labour's Lost* is published; for the first time, Shakespeare's name appears on a title page.

1599– Globe playhouse opens; *Julius Caesar* is performed on the Bankside, probably at the Globe; the *Passionate Pilgrim* is published, featuring poems by Christopher Marlowe, Sir Walter Raleigh, and Shakespeare.

1600– *As You Like It*, *Henry V*, and *Much Ado About Nothing* ordered "to be staied" from publication in the Stationer's Register; *As You Like It* is the only one of the three unpublished at the time of the First Folio; *Much Ado About Nothing*, *Henry V*, *A Midsummer*

Night's Dream, *The Merchant of Venice*, and *2 Henry IV* are published.

1601– John Shakespeare, the poet's father, dies; *The Phoenix and Turtle* is published as part of a collection called *Love's Martyr.*

1602– *Merry Wives of Windsor* comes out in a bad quarto; *Hamlet* is entered in the Stationers' Register.

1604– *Othello* and *Measure for Measure* are performed at court; *Hamlet* is published in a good quarto.

1606– *Coriolanus* and *Antony and Cleopatra* likely written in this year; *Macbeth* alludes to execution of Jesuit priest this year.

1608– *Antony and Cleopatra* entered in Stationer's Register but not published until 1623; Shakespeare's mother, Mary Arden, dies.

1609– Publication of *Troilus and Cressida*, the *Sonnets*, and *Pericles*.

1613– Shakespeare purchases the Blackfriars gatehouse.

1616– Shakespeare dies, apparently on his fifty-second birthday (April 23).

1619– Ten unauthorized quartos are published in Shakespeare's name.

1623– Shakespeare's wife, Anne, dies; Publication of the First Folio of Shakespeare's plays.

1632– Publication of Shakespeare's Second Folio with poem by twenty-four-year-old John Milton.

1634– Publication of *The Two Noble Kinsmen* by John Fletcher and William Shakespeare; this is the last of the Shakespeare first-edition quartos.

1662– Death of Shakespeare's daughter Judith at age seventy-seven.

1664– Publication of scarce Third Folio; The Great Fire of London two years later wiped out many copies, so that there are now more copies of the First Folio (around 230) than of the Third.

1670– Death of Shakespeare's granddaughter, Elizabeth Hall Nash, the last in Shakespeare's direct line of descent.

1685– Publication of Fourth (and last) Folio.

1765– Publication of Dr. Samuel Johnson's edition of Shakespeare.

1769– The Shakespeare Jubilee at Stratford.

1795– William Henry Ireland forges a mass of documents and two plays attributed by Shakespeare; these are exposed by Edmond Malone the following year.

1823– Q1 *Hamlet* surfaces in Barton, England, after being unknown for two hundred years.

1904– Q1 *Titus Andronicus* appears after a lapse of more than two centuries; this copy was found in Sweden and is the only copy known today.

1909– Mark Twain writes *Is Shakespeare Dead?* in which he disputes William Shakespeare's authorship of the works that go by his name.

1922– John Barrymore's *Hamlet*, perhaps the first production of the play to incorporate Freudian theory to the character of Hamlet.

1978–1984– The BBC television network broadcasts all of Shakespeare's plays.

1997– The *New Riverside Shakespeare* edition of William Shakespeare comes out.

2013– The *Arden Complete Collected Works of Shakespeare* includes *Double Falsehood* for the first time in any edition of Shakespeare. It is a play of possible part-Shakespearean authorship.

Chapter Notes

Chapter 1. The Bard of Avon

1. Author interview with Adeline Nall (1906–1996), November 1991.
2. Gareth Lloyd Evans, *The Upstart Crow: An Introduction to Shakespeare's Plays* (New York: J. M. Dent & Sons, 1982), 1.
3. *Henry IV, Part 2, The Signet Classic Shakespeare*, ed. Norman N. Holland (New York: Signet Classics, 1965), xxiii.
4. Robert Ornstein, *Shakespeare's Comedies: From Roman Farce to Romantic Mystery* (Newark, DE: University of Delaware Press, 1986), 14–19.
5. Edwin Wilson, ed., *Shaw on Shakespeare* (New York: Books For Libraries Press, 1961), 5.
6. S. Schoenbaum, *Shakespeare's Lives* (New York: The Clarendon Press, 1970), 547.
7. Ibid., 601.
8. Karl J. Holzknecht, *The Backgrounds of Shakespeare's Plays* (New York: American Book Co., 1950), 188.
9. M. Mahood, *Shakespeare's Wordplay* (London: Routledge, 1957), 56.
10. Andrew Gurr, "The Shakespearean Stage," *The Norton Shakespeare*, ed. Stephen Greenblatt, et. al. (New York: Norton, 1997), 3282.
11. *The Reader's Encyclopedia of Shakespeare*, Oscar James Campbell and Edward G. Quinn, eds. (New York: Thomas Y. Crowell, 1996), 668.
12. Ornstein, 36.

Chapter 2. The Age of Shakespeare

1. Nevil Truman, *Historical Costume* (Chicago: Pitman, 1944), 54.

2. Karl J. Holzknecht, *The Backgrounds of Shakespeare's Plays* (New York: American Book Company, 1950), 85.
3. Charles Boyce, *Shakespeare A to Z: The Essential Reference to His Plays, His Poems, His Life and Times, and More* (New York: Dell Publishing, 1991), 296.
4. Ian Wilson, *Shakespeare the Evidence: Unlocking the Mysteries of the Man and His Work* (New York: St. Martin's Press, 1993), 453.
5. Holzknecht, p. 32, and S. Schoenbaum, *Shakespeare's Lives* (New York: Clarendon Press, 1970), 73.
6. Wilson, 66.
7. Boyce, 242–243.
8. Holzknecht, 25.
9. Boyce, 600.
10. Boyce, 524.
11. Wilson, 317.
12. Bernard Beckerman, *Shakespeare at the Globe* (New York: MacMillan Co., 1962), 12.
13. Ibid., xii.
14. Boyce, 528.
15. Ibid., 615.
16. Sir Sidney Lee, *A Life of William Shakespeare* (New York: MacMillan Co., 1927), 517.

Chapter 3. The Poems and Sonnets

1. David Bevington, *The Complete Works of Shakespeare*, 4th ed. (New York: HarperCollins, 1992), 1578.
2. Charles Boyce, *Shakespeare A to Z: The Essential Reference to His Plays, His Poems, His Life and Times, and More* (New York: Dell Publishing, 1991), 314.
3. Ibid., 502.
4. S. Schoenbaum, *Shakespeare's Lives* (Oxford: Oxford University Press, 1970), 519.

Chapter 4. Shakespeare's History Plays

1. Kenneth Muir, *Shakespeare the Professional and Related Studies* (Totowa, NJ: Rowman and Littlefield, 1973), 77.
2. David Bevington, *The Complete Works of Shakespeare*, Fourth Edition (New York: HarperCollins, 1992), 539.
3. Muir, 77.
4. G. Blakemore Evans, general editor, et. al., *The Riverside Shakespeare* (Boston: Houghton Mifflin, 1997), 1926.
5. Bonnie Szumski, et al., eds., *Readings on the Comedies, William Shakespeare, The Greenhaven Press Literary Companion to British Literature* (San Diego: Greenhaven Press, 1997), 140.

Chapter 5. Shakespeare's Comedies

1. G. Blakemore Evans, general editor, et al., *The Riverside Shakespeare* (Boston: Houghton Mifflin Company, 1997), 80–82.
2. Robert Ornstein, *Shakespeare's Comedies: From Romantic Farce to Romantic Mystery* (Newark, DE: University of Delaware Press, 1986), 14; 251.
3. Douglas Brode, *Shakespeare in the Movies: From the Silent Era to Shakespeare in Love* (New York: Oxford University Press, 2000), 24.
4. Charles Boyce, *Shakespeare A to Z: The Essential Reference to His Plays, His Poems, His Life and Times, and More* (New York: Dell Publishing, 1991), 607.
5. Sir Sidney Lee, *A Life of William Shakespeare* (New York: MacMillan Co., 1927), 246–247.
6. Ibid., 6–7, 282–283.
7. Boyce, 607.
8. Ibid., 35.
9. Ibid., 451.
10. Evans, 21.

11. Boyce, 440.
12. Sylvan Barnet, ed., *The Signet Classic Shakespeare* (New York: New American Library, 1972), p. 1052. See also G. Harold Metz, "Wonne is 'Lost, Quite Lost,'" *Modern Language Studies*, 16, ii, (Spring 1986), 3–12.

Chapter 6. Shakespeare Hits His Stride: *A Midsummer Night's Dream*

1. John Dover Wilson and Sir Arthur Quiller-Couch, eds., *The Cambridge New Shakespeare: A Midsummer Night's Dream* (Cambridge: Cambridge University Press, 1969), xix.
2. Louis B. Wright and Virginia A. LaMar, eds., *The Folger Library General Reader's Shakespeare: A Midsummer Night's Dream* (New York: Washington Square Press, 1961), xiii.
3. G. Blakemore Evans, general editor, et al., *The Riverside Shakespeare* (Boston: Houghton Mifflin Company, 1997), 252.
4. Brian Vickers, *The Artistry of Shakespeare's Prose* (London: Methuen Co., 1968), 433.
5. E. K. Chambers and Edith Rickert, eds., *The Arden Shakespeare: A Midsummer Night's Dream* (Boston: D.C. Heath & Co., 1917), 169.
6. Charles Boyce, *Shakespeare A to Z: The Essential Reference to His Plays, His Poems, His Life and Times, and More* (New York: Dell Publishing, 1991), 607.
7. M. H. Abrams, general editor, "The Rose of the World," *The Norton Anthology of English Literature* (New York: W.W. Norton & Company, Inc., 1962), 1569.

Chapter 7. *Romeo and Juliet*: The Last Word on First Love

1. Douglas Brode, *Shakespeare in the Movies: From the Silent Era to Shakespeare in Love* (New York: Oxford University Press, 2000), 42–43.
2. G. Blakemore Evans, general editor, et al., *The Riverside Shakespeare* (Boston: Houghton Mifflin Company, 1997), 1145.
3. Kenneth Muir, *Shakespeare the Professional and Related Studies* (Totowa, NJ: Rowman and Littlefield, 1973), 92.
4. Robert Adger Law, *The Arden Shakespeare: Romeo and Juliet* (New York: DC Heath & Co., 1916), 218.
5. Thomas Marc Parrott, ed., *Shakespeare: Twenty-Three Plays and the Sonnets* (New York: Charles Scribner's Sons, 1953), 163.
6. Law, 218.
7. Edwin Wilson, ed., *Shaw on Shakespeare* (New York: Books For Libraries Press, 1961), 179.
8. Muir, 93.
9. Ibid., 96.
10. Ibid., 226.

Chapter 8. *Julius Caesar*: The Misnamed Tragedy?

1. Stephen Greenblatt, et. al., eds., *The Norton Shakespeare: Based on the Oxford Edition* (New York: W.W. Norton & Company, 1997), 1531.
2. Brian Vickers, *The Artistry of Shakespeare's Prose* (London: Methuen & Co. Ltd., 1968), 433.
3. Ibid., 241.
4. Charles Boyce, *Shakespeare A to Z: The Essential Reference to His Plays, His Poems, His Life and Times, and More* (New York: Dell Publishing, 1991), 463.
5. Ibid., 513.

Chapter 9. Shakespeare's Incomparable *Hamlet*

1. E. K. Chambers, ed., Walter Morris Hart, American editor, C.H. Herford, series general editor, *Hamlet, the Arden Shakespeare* (New York: DC Heath, 1917), 225, note d.
2. Greenblatt, Stephen, et.al., eds, *The Norton Shakespeare Based on the Oxford Text* (New York: W.W. Norton and Co., 1997), 3297.
3. Brian Vickers, *The Artistry of Shakespeare's Prose* (London: Methuen & Co. Ltd., 1968), 248–53, 443, notes 4 and 8.
4. Edward Hubler, ed., *The Signet Classic Hamlet* (New York: New American Library, 1963), 176.
5. G. B. Harrison, *Shakespeare's Major Plays and the Sonnets*, 3rd ed. (New York: Harcourt Brace and World, 3rd ed., 1958), 5.
6. Kenneth Muir, *The Singularity of Shakespeare and Other Essays* (Liverpool: Liverpool University Press, 1977), 110–111.
7. George Lyman Kittredge, ed., *Hamlet* (Boston: Ginn and Company, 1939), 132.
8. Michael A. Morrison, *John Barrymore, Shakespearean Actor* (Cambridge: Cambridge University Press, 1997), 129–132.
9. Muir, 51.

Chapter 10. Shakespeare's Other Tragedies

1. S. Schoenbaum, *Shakespeare's Lives* (Oxford: Clarendon Press, 1991), 357–358.
2. G. P. V. Akrigg, *Shakespeare & the Earl of Southampton* (Cambridge: Harvard University Press, 1968), 254–255.
3. Sir Sidney Lee, *A Life of William Shakespeare* (New York: The MacMillan Company, 1927), 374.

4. Errol Hill, *Shakespeare in Sable: A History of Black Shakespearean Actors* (Amherst: University of Massachusetts Press, 1984), 126.
5. Ibid., 128.
6. David J. Harkness and R. Gerald McMurtry, *Lincoln's Favorite Poets* (Knoxville: University of Tennessee Press, 1959), 26.
7. Isaac Asimov, *Asimov's Guide to Shakespeare Volume One* (Garden City, NY: Doubleday, 1970), 417.
8. Sylvan Barnet, ed., *Signet Classic Shakespeare* Titus Andronicus (New York: New American Library, 1977), xxi.
9. G. Blakemore Evans, general editor, et al., *The Riverside Shakespeare* (Boston: Houghton Mifflin Company, 1997), 1490.
10. Brian Vickers, *The Artistry of Shakespeare's Prose* (London: Methuen Co. Ltd., 1968), 433.
11. Ibid., 377.
12. Louis B. Wright and Virginia A. LaMar, eds., *The Folger Library General Reader's Shakespeare* Coriolanus (New York: Washington Square Press, 1969), vii.
13. Richard L. Sterne, *John Gielgud Directs Richard Burton in* Hamlet: *A Journal of Rehearsals* (New York: Random House, 1967).

Chapter 11. Not Exactly This or That: The Romances

1. Gerald Eades Bentley, "Shakespeare and the Blackfriars Theatre," *Shakespeare Survey I* (Cambridge: Cambridge University Press, 1948), 38–50.
2. G. Blakemore Evans, general editor, et al., *The Riverside Shakespeare* (Boston: Houghton Mifflin, 1997), 1565.
3. Rhona Silverbush and Sami Plotkin, *Speak the Speech: Shakespeare's Monologues Illuminated* (Faber and Faber, 2002), 833–835.

4. Ifor Evans, *The Language of Shakespeare's Plays* (London: Methuen & Co. Ltd, 1966), 204–205.
5. Mark Twain, "Is Shakespeare Dead?" *The Complete Essays of Mark Twain*, Charles Neider, ed. (Garden City: Doubleday and Company, Inc., 1963), 430.
6. Hallett Smith, "Cymbeline," *The Riverside Shakespeare*, G. Blakemore Evans, general editor (Boston: Houghton Mifflin, 1997), 1690.

Chapter 12. Shakespeare: Then and Now

1. Ron Rosenbaum, *The Shakespeare Wars: Clashing Scholars, Public Fiascoes, Palace Coups* (New York: Random House, 2006), 179–180.
2. Hugh Craig, "George Chapman, John Hereford, William Shakespeare and 'A Lover's Complaint,'" *Shakespeare Quarterly* 202 (Washington, DC: Folger Shakespeare Library, 2012), 147–175.
3. The idea that Shakespeare wanted to be read as well as acted is an old one. For a discussion of early thinking in this vein, see G. G. Greenwood, *Is There A Shakespeare Problem?* (London: John Lane, 1916), 441–449. See also, Lukas Erne, "Shakespeare and the Publication of His Plays," *Shakespeare Quarterly* 53 (Washington, DC: Folger Shakespeare Library, 2002), 1–20.
4. James Shapiro, ed., *Shakespeare in America* (New York: Library of America, 2014).
5. G. G. Greenwood, *Is There A Shakespeare Problem?* (London: John Lane, 1916), xi-xii.
6. For a fascinating look at many of the old sixteenth- and seventeenth-century quartos, visit: www.bl.uk/treasures/shakespeare/homepage/html.

LITERARY TERMS

allegorical—Relating to allegory; when something is designed to represent or symbolize something else.

alliteration—The repetition of words beginning with the same consonant.

allusion—A seemingly incidental mention of something that is, in reality, designed to hint at a much deeper meaning.

anapestic—A form of poetic meter wherein two unstressed syllables precede a stressed syllable.

blank verse—Unrhymed iambic pentameter

canon—The body of work by an author.

complaint poem—A long poem in which a lady grieves over the faithlessness of her lover.

conceit—This word got around in Shakespeare's day. It could mean idea, figure of speech, or conception of something. In one of his soliloquies, Hamlet uses the word to mean something like a blend of conception and arrogance, but usually our idea of the word and Shakespeare's are two different things.

couplet—Two successive lines of verse that are joined in some way (usually by rhyme).

end-stopped—A line of poetry that is a complete sentence (i.e., when one line does not continue into the next line).

farce—A comedy that is all chance or accident driven (as opposed to character driven).

foil—A character who is nearly the direct opposite of the hero or heroine of a story. Laertes and Fortinbras, for example, are foils to Hamlet.

folio—A book printed from leaves that are folded in half. Each leaf makes two separate pages.

foreshadow—A literary technique whereby something that takes place early in a story evolves into a significant development as the story progresses.

hyperbole—An extreme exaggeration.

iambic—A metrical foot of poetry or verse has an unstressed syllable preceding a stressed syllable.

metaphor—A figure of speech in which a comparison is made between two words or phrases that have no literal relationship.

octave (or octet)—A poetic stanza or group of lines that is eight lines in length.

octavo—A book printed from leaves folded three times, making eight pages.

oxymoron—A figure of speech where two opposite terms or ideas are combined (e.g., "a deafening silence").

pentameter—A line of poetic verse possessing five metrical feet (ten syllables).

personification—A figure of speech in which an inanimate object is treated as, or compared to, a living thing.

prologue—A short introduction to the work at hand. There are five prologues in Shakespeare's plays. Probably the most famous is that of *Romeo and Juliet*.

pun—A form of wordplay wherein a joke is made out of words that have the same sound (and perhaps even the same spelling) but different meanings.

quarto—A book printed from leaves folded twice, making four separate pages.

quatrain—A poetic stanza or group of lines that is four lines in length.

quibble—A pun, a play on words, or verbal means of evading a point.

sestet—A poetic stanza or group of lines that is six lines in length.

sibilance—A gathering of *s* sounds in the space of a line or two of literature.

simile—A figure of speech in which a comparison is made between two words or phrases through use of the terms "like" or "as."

soliloquy—A dramatic device wherein one character alone appears to speak to himself, thereby revealing his innermost thoughts and feelings to the audience.

sonnet—A poem that consists of fourteen lines of verse, typically written in iambic pentameter.

spondee—A metric foot consisting of two stressed syllables.

stanza—A portion of a poem divided from the larger poem via a recurring pattern of meter or rhyme.

symbol—Something that stands for, represents, or suggests another idea or thing.

symbolism—The representation of things by use of symbols.

tercet—A poetic stanza or group of lines that is three lines in length.

tetralogy—A series of four connected works.

tetrameter—A line of poetic verse possessing four metrical feet (eight syllables).

theme—A distinctive quality or concern in one or more works of fiction.

trimeter—A line of poetic verse possessing three metrical feet (six syllables).

trochaic—A metric foot possessing a stressed syllable before an unstressed syllable.

SURVIVING WORKS OF WILLIAM SHAKESPEARE

Comedies

All's Well That Ends Well
As You Like It
The Comedy of Errors
Love's Labour's Lost
Measure for Measure
The Merchant of Venice
The Merry Wives of Windsor
A Midsummer Night's Dream
Much Ado About Nothing
Taming of the Shrew
Troilus and Cressida
Twelfth Night
Two Gentlemen of Verona
Histories
Henry IV, part 1
Henry IV, part 2
Henry V
Henry VI, part 1
Henry VI, part 2
Henry VI, part 3
Henry VIII
King John
Richard II
Richard III

Tragedies

Antony and Cleopatra
Coriolanus

Hamlet
Julius Caesar
King Lear
Macbeth
Othello
Romeo and Juliet
Timon of Athens
Titus Andronicus

Romances

Cymbeline
Pericles
The Tempest
The Two Noble Kinsmen (coauthor with John Fletcher)
The Winter's Tale

Poetry

A Lover's Complaint
The Phoenix and Turtle
The Rape of Lucrece
Venus and Adonis
The *Sonnets*

Further Reading

Bloom, Harold. *William Shakespeare's* Hamlet. Broomall, PA: Chelsea House, 1995.

Crystal, David and Ben. *Oxford Illustrated Shakespeare Dictionary*. Oxford, England: Oxford University Press, 2015.

Crystal, Ben. *Shakespeare on Toast*: *Getting a Taste of the Bard*. New York: Icon Books Ltd, 2012.

Dutton-Downer, Leslie, and Alan Riding. *Essential Shakespeare Handbook*. New York: DK, 2013.

McMurty, Jo. *Shakespeare Films in the Classroom*. New York: Shoestring Press, 1994.

Proudfoot, Richard, et. al. ed. *The Arden Shakespeare Complete Works*. New York: Bloomsbury Publishing, 2014.

The Shakespeare Book: Big Ideas Simply Explained. New York: DK Publishing, 2015.

Shapiro, James. ed. *Shakespeare in America: From the Revolution to Now*. New York: Library of America, 2014.

Websites

The Complete Works of William Shakespeare
shakespeare.mit.edu/works.html
Includes the text of Shakespeare's major plays and poetry.

Shakespeare Online
www.shakespeare-online.com/
Provides summary, analysis, biography, and trivia.

Digging for the Curtain
www.literarygenius.info/william-shakespeare-london.htm
Information concerning recent excavations and archaeological finds of such London sites as the Rose, the Curtain, the Theatre, and Globe playhouses.

Shakespeare's England
www.shakespearesengland.co.uk/category/maps/
Maps pinpointing places of interest in Shakespeare's life and career.

Digital Media and Teaching Shakespeare
www.edutopia.org/teaching-shakespeare-digital-media
Teachers utilize music and video technology to teach Shakespeare in high school.

50 Popular Phrases That Came From Shakespeare
www.independent.co.uk/arts-entertainment/books/news/william-shakespeare-birthday-50-popular-phrases-that-came-from-the-famous-playwright-10198259.html
Everyday expressions that we owe to Shakespeare's plays and poems.

Shakespeare in Quarto
www.bl.uk/treasures/shakespeare/homepage.html
Copies in various editions of twenty-one of Shakespeare's plays found at the British Library.

Index

T

W

Y